Lord, Deliver Us *from the* EVIL

Rev. Clifford Little

ISBN 978-1-63903-276-1 (paperback)
ISBN 978-1-63903-275-4 (digital)

Christian Faith Publishing
832 Park Avenue
Meadville, PA 16335
www.christianfaithpublishing.com

Printed in the United States of America

Contents

Foreword

This book comes from a pastor's heart. Cliff Little is a man who heard the Lord call him and responded by decades of dedicated service to God's people. When he reads the Scripture text for his sermons, you almost get the impression that he was an eyewitness to the story it tells. You know he has prayerfully lived into the passage, and the Holy Spirit's presence is palpable.

The chapters of this book come across with that same directness and authenticity. Preachers have a powerful position from which to influence their parishioners, essentially for ill as well as for good. The prestige of the preacher in the African American community, from the earliest days, has been particularly great. Cliff's congregants know that they can trust him because of his great love for God's Word and his unconditional love for them. He is as gentle as a lamb with them personally and as strong as a lion in defense of God's Word.

You will find in this study a healthy balance between the importance of spiritual warfare and practical advice on how to avoid the corrupt influences of our lost and dying world. Chapter 6 warns against allowing political agendas to get in the way of the biblical message. Chapters 8–10 respond to the secular culture's attacks on the Church, the Scriptures, and the traditional family. Chapter 11, on "What We Must Do" to overcome the evil, is especially powerful. Pastor Little emphasizes using the full armor of God, including watching and praying, along with fasting (an all too often neglected discipline).

As you read this book, test the spirits, as Cliff advises. I did, and I found that this man has a rich fountain of wisdom earned by years of building his life and ministry on the pure manna of "every Word that proceeds out of the mouth of the Lord."

John Marson Dunaway, PhD
Professor emeritus, Mercer University
Founder, Beloved Community of Macon, Georgia

Preface

We are born into a world of evil. The prophet Isaiah said in Isaiah 9:2, "The people who walked in darkness have seen a great light: they that dwell in the land of the shadow of death, upon them hath the light shined." **I am convinced that the earth is the "land of the shadow of death." Death is all around us. Sickness, sorrow, trials, and tribulations are all around us. Devils, demons, and evil spirits are all around us.** Evil is an integral part of life on the earth. But there is hope; **there is hope and help for "deliverance from the evil."**

This book was conceived in my spirit in the early 1990s when I stepped out as a middle-aged minister to pastor one of God's churches. Over the course of time and during my lifetime, God had shown me a lot of evil that is present in the world and in the church. **I felt that God had impressed it upon my spirit to, at some point, write a book and entitle it *Lord, Deliver Us from the Evil*,** which was inspired by two of the prayers that were prayed by our Lord and Savior, Jesus Christ.

I never shared my intentions with anyone, not family nor any of my friends, some of whom were already writing and publishing their books. **One day in the mid-1990s, during one of our revival services, a minister friend of**

mine prophesied that I would write a book. I simply responded, "Amen! Amen!" and "Praise the Lord!" but I didn't share with him or the others that God had put it in my heart to do just that. I have been praying about the time for the book, and now I feel that the time is now.

So I am writing this book to encourage, enlighten, inspire, and hopefully help Christian followers and believers to be aware of the forces of evil that are around us in the world and in the church and to fight more effectively to be delivered from the power of that evil.

As mentioned earlier, the title for this book is based on the prayer that our Lord and Savior, Jesus Christ, taught us in Matthew 6:13 when He said for us to pray in this manner: "And lead us not into temptation, but deliver us from evil" and **also the prayer that He prayed in John 17:15** when He prayed to Father God, "I pray not that Thou should take them out of the world, **but that Thou should keep them from the evil."** Jesus knew that evil was all around us in this world, and that we should address it in our prayers and ask our heavenly Father to "deliver us from the evil."

There is hope, and there is help for "deliverance from the evil," but we must be knowledgeable, aware, and sometimes "problem specific" in identifying and acknowledging "the evil" or "the problem" or the spirit/devil that we are dealing with so that we can be delivered.

Scriptural quotes and references are from the King James Version Bible **(KJV)** and the New King James Version Bible **(NKJV)**. I relied primarily on the KJV Bible, so no doubt, you will at times notice the unique spelling and phrasing of the KJV because I love it and chose not to shy away from its rendering of the Holy Writ. I pray that the uniqueness of the KJV does not detract from anyone's acceptance of the text or the message being conveyed in that passage of the book.

There are several places in this book where specific references to "satan" are in lowercase letters. I am aware that "proper names" are to be capitalized, but this is an **intentional** effort on my part to not give the devil any glory.

There are also instances when the word "Church" is capitalized, especially when referring to the universal or general ecclesiastical body of Christian believers. **This is similar to what we do when we refer to proper nouns such as the Supreme Court or the Presidency of the United States of America.** The same holds true when referring to the **"Bible"** or the **"Word"** of God or the **"Scriptures."** I hope that no one is offended by thinking that these are typographical errors, etc., and I pray that this book is a blessing to all who read it.

Chapter 1

The Causes of Evil

The first thing you want to do to be "delivered from the evil" is to recognize the presence and the causes of evil. Apostle Paul reminded us in the book of Ephesians that we don't "wrestle against flesh and blood, but against principalities, against powers, against the rulers of the darkness of this world, against spiritual wickedness in high places" (Ephesians 6:12).

This passage reveals to us that our struggles are not so much with people ("flesh and blood") but with spirits. **Often times, there is a spirit or spirits behind the person or the problem that we're having trouble with.** Paul earlier identified this spirit in Ephesians 2:2 as satan or the devil or "the prince of the power of the air."

Satan and his demons (fallen angels) rule in the atmosphere around the earth and on the earth. If you are familiar with your Bible, you probably know that **satan started a rebellion in heaven and was "cast out" of heaven and down to the earth, along with a third of the angels that**

rebelled with him (Isaiah 14:12–15 and Revelation 12:3–9).

> And there appeared another wonder in heaven; and behold a great red dragon, having seven heads and ten horns, and seven crowns upon his heads. And his tail drew the third part of the stars of heaven, and did cast them to the earth: and the dragon stood before the woman which was ready to be delivered, for to destroy her Child as soon as it was born. (Revelation 12:3–4)
>
> **And there was war in heaven:** Michael and his angels fought against the dragon; and the dragon fought and his angels, and prevailed not; neither was their place found any more in heaven. **And the great dragon was cast out, that old serpent, called the devil, and satan, which deceived the whole world: he was cast out into the earth, and his angels were cast out with him. (Revelation 12:7–9)**

Jesus said in Luke 10:18, "I beheld satan as lightening fall from heaven." When the devil arrived on earth, he began to lie and deceive and manipulate man and things on the earth. In the Gospel according to John, **Jesus told the Pharisees,**

> **You are of your father the devil,** and the lust of your father you will do. He was a murderer from the beginning, and abode not in the truth, because there is no truth in him. When he speaketh a lie he speaketh of his own: for he is a liar, and the father of it. (John 8:44)

Three areas of temptation

So the devil or demons or spirits are behind most of the evil that we are confronted with in the world. But of course, we can't blame everything on the devil alone. In order to be effective, satan must make contact with something that's in us. **John, in the First Epistle of John, tells us that there are three areas that satan gets to us or three categories of sin: "the lust of the flesh, the lust of the eyes, and the pride of life"** which is "not of the Father, but is of the world" (1 John 2:16).

Apostle Paul was aware of his (our) vulnerability to the flesh and the possibility of us being "led" or misled by the devil and commit errors or "sin" because of the weaknesses of our flesh. Paul said,

> I know that in me, that is in my flesh dwelleth no good thing… **When I would do good, evil is present with me, so that**

I cannot do the good that I would" (Romans 7:18–21)

In the Garden of Eden, Adam and Eve were victimized by the devil's tempting them in the three areas or categories of sin. The Bible says in Genesis 3:6,

> And when the woman saw that the tree was good for food [the "lust of the flesh"], and that it was pleasant to the eyes [the "lust of the eyes"], and a tree to be desired to make one wise [the "pride of life"], she took of the fruit thereof, and did eat, and gave also to her husband with her; and he did eat.

They were lied to and deceived by the devil through something that was in their flesh. Beware of your flesh or the flesh of somebody else.

Even our Lord and Savior, Jesus Christ, was "tempted" in all three of these areas. The Bible says that **He was "in all points tempted like as we are, yet without sin" (Hebrews 4:15).** In the book of Matthew, chapter 4, the Bible says,

> And when He had fasted forty days and forty nights, He was afterwards an hungered [or hungry]. And **when the tempter came to Him,** he said, If Thou be the Son

> of God, command that these stones be made bread. (Matthew 4:2–3)

This was the area of the "lust of the flesh."

You are probably familiar with this story. The Bible says the devil did not stop there.

> Then the devil taketh Him up into the holy city, and setteth Him on a pinnacle of the temple; and saith unto Him, If Thou be the Son of God, cast Thyself down: for it is written, "He shall give His angels charge concerning thee: and in their arms they shall bear Thee up, lest at any time Thou dash Thy foot against a stone." (Matthew 4:5–6)

That is amazing but the devil knows Scripture too. He was quoting Psalm 91:11, and he was **tempting Jesus through the area of "the pride of life"** to show people how big and how important He was with angelic protection.

> Again, the devil taketh Him up into an exceeding high mountain, and **showed Him all the kingdoms of the world,** and the glory of them; And saith unto Him, All these will I give Thee, if Thou will fall down and worship me. (Matthew 4:8–9)

At this point, Jesus was being tempted in the area of "the lust of the eyes" ("What the eyes see, the eyes want."), **and He was, therefore, "in all points tempted like as we are, yet without sin."**

Satan does not care whether you know scriptures or whether you can quote scriptures as long as you don't practice the Scriptures properly or stand on what the Word of God says. **He was trying to deceive Jesus just like he deceived Adam and Eve in the garden of Eden.** Jesus stood His ground on the Word and told satan where to go and what to do: "Get thee hence, satan: for it is written, Thou shall worship the Lord thy God, and Him only shall thy serve" (Matthew 4:10).

Natural causes of evil

And of course, there are natural causes of "evil" or bad things. Ever since man sinned in the garden of Eden, bad things have been happening to the earth and to man. In Genesis 3:17–19, **when Adam sinned, God "cursed the ground"** and said man would reap or eat in "sorrow" of the ground "all the days of his life." God said, "Thorns and thistles shall it bring forth to thee… In the sweat of thy face shall thou eat bread, until thou return unto the ground; for out of it was thou taken: for dust thou are, and unto dust shall thou return."

Therefore, some sicknesses, afflictions, and infirmities have natural causes, but there are some that are caused by spirits or by the devil himself, such as in Mark 5 when Jesus met a "man with an unclean spirit." Jesus spoke to the spirit that was in the man and said, "What is thy name?"

The spirit answered Jesus, saying, "My name is Legion; for we are many" (Mark 5:9). Spirits were causing this man to be sick and tormented.

In Luke 13:11, there was a woman with "a spirit of infirmity" for eighteen years, and Jesus healed her, saying, "Woman, thou are loosed from thine infirmity." And in John 5:5, when Jesus went up to Jerusalem to the pool of Bethesda, **the Bible says there was "a certain man there which had an infirmity thirty eight years," and Jesus healed him,** saying to the man, "Rise, take up thy bed and walk."

No matter what the cause (natural, spiritual, or demonic), everybody is going to have to deal with some kind of evil or problem or negative situation in life. Apostle Paul reminds us in 1 Corinthians 10:13,

> There has no temptation taken you but such as is common to man: but God is faithful, who will not suffer you to be tempted above that you are able; but will with the temptation (or the trouble, or the problem) also make a way to escape, that you may be able to bear it.

That just reminds us that "God is able," and anything that He doesn't save us from, He'll give us the grace to go through.

The love of money

The Bible tells us that, "The love of money is the root of all evil: which while some coveted after, they have erred from the faith, and pierced themselves through with many sorrows" (1 Timothy 6:10).

Satan uses the "love of money" to tempt us in all three areas of temptation: "the lust of the flesh, the lust of the eyes, and the pride of life." Apostle Paul told Timothy to "charge them that are rich in this world, that they be not high-minded, nor trust in uncertain riches, but in the living God, who giveth us richly all things to enjoy" (1 Timothy 6:17).

Christians, ministers, pastors, and other church leaders have been tempted by the "love of money" or the love of the "things" that money can buy (just like people of the world). **I am convinced that the love of money or the love of power, prestige, or "things" have clouded the minds of many Christians**, including pastors and other church leaders and have caused them to "fall away" and be unfaithful to the gospel of Jesus Christ.

In the Gospel of Matthew, **a rich young man came to Jesus** and asked Him, **"What good thing shall I do, that I may have eternal life?"**

Jesus answered him by saying, "If you will be perfect, go and sell what you have, and give it to the poor, and you shall have treasure in heaven: **and come and follow Me" (Matthew 19:16–21).**

The Bible says that when the young ruler heard that, **"He went away sorrowful: for he had great riches."** Jesus responded to His disciples, "Verily I say unto you, that a rich man shall hardly enter into the kingdom of heaven" (Matthew 19:22–23).

He continued, "And again I say unto you, it is easier for a camel to go through the eye of a needle, than for a rich man to enter into the kingdom of God." **Jesus did not say that a rich man could not be saved but that it would be very hard.**

Capitalism and the "free market" system

In Proverbs 23:4, Solomon, the wisest man to live upon the earth, advised us to **"labor not to be rich: cease from thine own wisdom."** Unfortunately, capitalism and the "free market" system sometimes breed greed. People are trying to gain wealth anyway that they can: breaking laws, cheating on taxes, "insider trading," and "price gouging," trying to get rich or gain wealth.

God is not against us being monetarily rich, but He doesn't want getting rich or accumulating wealth to be our life goal because He knows that it will "pierce us through with many sorrows" and lead to corruption. **If we are faithful to God and follow godly principles, we will prosper and be successful in our endeavors, including financial success,** and not only will our needs be met, but we will also have an excess ("overflow"). Because we have "kept the faith," along with that excess or "overflow," we will also have the peace of God. **Solomon said, "The blessing of the Lord, it maketh rich, and He addeth no sorrow with it" (Proverbs 10:22).**

Chapter 2

Strategies for Overcoming the Evil

The first thing you want to do when dealing with a specific problem or situation is identify the cause or what's behind the problem. Is it natural, or is it caused by a spirit or demons, as mentioned earlier? If a person is hungry, you may simply need to "feed them." **Some sicknesses or physical ailments and infirmities will heal through prayer and a natural "healing process" of time; others may need prayer and medicinal intervention. Remember, God made medicines too.** "The earth is the Lord's and the fullness thereof" (Psalm 24:1a).

Secondly, if it is determined that a problem, a sickness, or a situation is caused by a spirit, then you will need to deal with it in spiritual ways. I remember once when my late father was in the hospital being treated for cancer (God rest his soul). One time, I went into his room, and he was delirious and out of his head. He was mimicking the voice of an old landlord that we had rented from when I was a child. **I quickly recognized that it was a spirit that had gotten into his spirit,** so instead of calling the nurse to adjust his medications, etc., **I spoke to the spirit that was manifesting and commanded the spirit to "come out of him" and leave him alone.** Well, he quickly settled down and returned to his natural state of mind. Needless to say, he also recovered his health and was released from the hospital soon thereafter.

On another occasion, when dealing with a situation in my own home with afflictions in the house, I began to suspect that the devil or spirits were involved. So I decided to stand guard and sleep in the room where the problem was occurring. Sure enough, in the wee hours of the night, I was suddenly awakened by the most hideous, shrill, screeching, and captivating sound that I had ever heard. **It was a spirit that had entered the room.** This spirit was satanic and demonic, and **all I could do was call out to "Jesus!"** As I called out "Jesus," **I regained my ability to speak, and I began to "bind up" and "cast" the spirit out of the room and out of our house.** We've never had a problem with that spirit again.

Some of you will say that I was only "dreaming" or that it was "just my imagination," but I'm saying to you that the situation was real, and the spirit that entered the room with me that night was real. We also need to acknowledge that satan (the devil) is real, and satanic and demonic spirits are real. First Peter 5:8–9 tells us, "Be sober, be vigilant; because your adversary the devil, as a roaring lion, walketh about, seeking whom he may devour: Whom resist steadfast in the faith."

Sometimes, when dealing with spirits, you need to have two or three other "believers" with you. There is a reason why Jesus sent the apostles and the other "seventy disciples" out "two and two" (Luke 10:1). The Scriptures tell us that "One can chase a thousand but two, ten thousand" (Deuteronomy 32:30).

I've had times when I've had to cast devils out of people and also out of homes. I remember one time there was this woman who was a member of our church. She had two young kids who had toys that her children would play with and leave out at night. Well, on some nights late in the wee hours, when her children had gone to bed, there would be sounds in her living room, and the toys would begin to move around as if someone was playing with them. The lights were out and her kids were in bed. **It was clear to me that her house was being invaded by a spirit, an "uninvited guest."**

I don't know what had happened in that house to draw that child's spirit or to draw a ghost into that house to play with the children's toys. Perhaps some little child had died there under tragic or sudden circumstances. **My wife and I went to the house (at night as "fate" would have it).** I was a little leery about that, but we spoke to the spirit, commanded it to leave the house and not to come back.

Sure enough, as we spoke to the spirit and called it out, some strange activity started happening in the house. The woman suddenly felt an extremely hot sensation. There was a strange gust of air that gently moved her screen door. We believe the spirit was leaving the house. **The woman said that after that, she was able to sleep peacefully and without any more disturbances of that kind.**

When people die, their spirits go either to heaven to "be present with the Lord" (2 Corinthians 5:8) or to hell (hades) to wait for the judgment (Revelation 20:11–12). **Whether devils, demons, or ghosts, spirits are real**, and we need to learn how to deal with them when we encounter them.

Chapter 3

Discerning the Evil

In order to effectively deal with the evil that is in the world and that is all around us, **we must learn to "discern the spirits."** There is a supernatural **"manifestation" gift of the Spirit called the "gift of discerning of spirits,"** which God can anoint us with for specific situations and circumstances. **Unfortunately, God does not show us everything supernaturally**. Sometimes, we have to apply godly wisdom, knowledge, and understanding in order to correctly discern what kind of spirits or forces we are dealing with.

Hebrews 5:13–14 tells us that discerning of spirits is not for babies.

> For every one that uses milk is unskillful in the word of righteousness: for he is a babe. But strong meat belongs to them that are of full age, even those who by reason of use have their senses exercised to discern both good and evil.

First John 4:1 says, "Beloved, believe not every spirit, but try the spirits whether they are of God: because many false prophets have gone out into the world."

One problem that we encounter when trying to truthfully discern the spirits is the result of an error that has been taught in the Church. **Most of us probably were taught or have heard the phrase "try the spirit by the spirit." Well, I have learned that is not the way to "try a spirit."** Spirits will deceive you; they will lie and agree with one another just to persuade you or to accomplish whatever their purpose is.

You can have a whole lot of spirits feeling good and agreeing with one another, and they all can be wrong. It happened a lot in the Bible. Remember Elijah and the 450 prophets of Baal in the "contest on Mt. Carmel" (1 Kings 18:22–40). Sometimes whole churches, denominations, or groups of people can be deceived by spirits feeling good and in agreement with one another, but they all can be wrong.

Please take note of "Micaiah's prophecy" in 2 Chronicles 18:3–34. Lying prophets cost Ahab his life in a battle he should not have fought and **almost cost Jehoshaphat his life as well.** In verse 21, a "lying spirit" told God that he would "go and be a lying spirit in the mouth of all Ahab's prophets." **Beware of trying a spirit simply by another spirit.**

Well, what are we supposed to do? The answer is we are supposed to "try the spirit" by the Word of God. In Matthew chapter four, when Jesus was tried and tempted by the devil after fasting forty days and forty nights, He gave us a good example as to how to handle the devil or any other kind of spirit. **Jesus kept telling the devil, "It is written."**

When satan said, "If Thou be the Son of God, command these stones that they be turned into bread," Jesus answered satan by speaking the Word of God to him: "Man shall not live by bread alone but by every Word that proceeds out of the mouth of God" (Matthew 4:4). **After each temptation, Jesus overcame the temptation and kept the devil in check by speaking and applying the Word of God: "It is written."**

That's what we should do. In order to "try the spirits" and correctly and truthfully "discern" the spirits, **we should apply the "Word test."** See if the spirit can pass the "Word test," or see if the spirit is telling you the truth. The **Scriptures let us know that in 1 John chapter 5.**

After telling us to "try the spirits" in 1 John chapter 4, **John tells us in 1 John 5:7, "There are three that bear record in heaven, the Father, the Word, and the Holy Ghost: and these three are one."** The Spirit (the Father and the Holy Ghost) must always agree with the Word. **Try the spirits by the Word of God.**

The fallacy of "trying the spirit by the spirit"

Therein lies the problem. Many people have not realized the fallacy of "trying the spirit by the spirit" and consequently they are prone to make more mistakes in life and even in ministry, some of them quite serious. **Just be-cause you feel good about something or just because someone**

is agreeing with you about something does not in and of itself mean that it is of God or that it is okay.

I've known ministers and pastors who felt strongly that God was leading them to do a certain thing. They felt good about it "in their spirit," and maybe there were church folks and other church members and friends who were in agreement with them about what they were planning to do. In the end, even though they made great sacrifices, spent lots of money, and sometimes worked on it for years, the thing didn't work out. **I believe that in most of those cases, the preacher was being misled by a "spirit of error" or by their own "feelings."**

Some elderly senior pastors that I used to hang around used to say, **"Where God gives vision, He makes provision."** I believe that is a true statement because Apostle Paul tells us in the book of Philippians, "My God shall supply all your need according to His riches in glory by Christ Jesus" (Philippians 4:19). **When we are in His will and doing what He wants us to do, God certainly will provide.**

I had a minister friend who was persuaded that God wanted him to start his own church. He had been pretty successful pastoring some of the local churches, but he was persuaded that God wanted him to start a church, so he started a church, started pastoring it, and worked diligently with it for years. **To my knowledge, the church that he started never grew to more than maybe six or seven members,** so being a friend of mine, I said to him one day, "Are you sure that God wanted you to "start" a church and "pastor" it?"

He said, "I know this is what God wanted me to do." **He was fully persuaded that he was doing what God wanted him to do, but the church never grew past that six or seven members.** He was not that old, but in his latter years, he began to have health issues, the "church" began to go down and finally became nonexistent. After a tragic accident, God took him home to be with the Lord. May God rest his soul.

My friend was sincere in what he was trying to do, but I believe he was "sincerely wrong" or being "misled." I believe that some of these "pastors" who started a church would have been better advised to bring their "ministry" under a larger church and under their personal pastor.

You can have all the "zeal" in the world and still be wrong. We can be "on fire" for God and feel like we are being "led by the Spirit" and still not be walking in "knowledge" or in the "truth" of God's Word. Apostle Paul talked about people who had a "zeal of God" but still were not saved. They had "zeal" but were not walking in the "knowledge" of God. **Paul said,**

> **For I bear them record that they have a zeal of God but not according to knowledge.** For they being ignorant of God's righteousness, and going about to establish their own righteousness, have not submitted themselves unto the righteousness of God. (Romans 10:2–3)

We must be very prayerful before we step out into ministry to make sure that's what God wants us to do, how He wants us to do it, and when does He want us to do it. **Remember David in 1 Chronicles chapter 17.** David had in his heart to build a house for the Lord, so he inquired of Nathan his prophet. At first, Nathan told David, "Go and do whatever is in thine heart; for God is with thee" (1 Chronicles 17:2). **They were "in agreement," but then God told Nathan, "Go and tell David thou shall not build Me a House to dwell in."**

God told David that his son Solomon was going to build Him a house, and David was humble enough and obedient enough to defer building the temple even though it was in his heart to do it. Building a "house for the Lord" or "starting a church for the Lord" is a good work, and a person may feel good about wanting to do that, but it may not be what the Lord wants them to do. **We must learn to "try the spirit" truthfully, even "try" our own spirit**, and then we must learn to be led by the Holy Spirit, which is the "Spirit of truth" (John 16:13).

There is a common saying in our church that "only what you do for Christ is going to last." I believe that is a true saying. The Bible tells us that there is a fire coming, and that fire is going to

> try every man's work of what sort it is. If any man's work abide which he has built thereupon, he shall receive a reward. **If any man's work shall be burned, he shall**

> **suffer loss: but he himself shall be saved; yet so as by fire.** (1 Corinthians 3:13–15)

Therefore, we will not receive an eternal reward for all of our works, even for some works that we thought were "good works." **We will only be rewarded for the works we've done for the right reasons and in accordance with the will of God.**

Chapter 4

Beware of Being "Misled" by People

Beware of following people and accepting everything that people say without question, even if they are prominent people, nationally and internationally known, and well established. **I have a saying that I use sometimes** in my effort to encourage people to not follow anybody blindly. I say to them, **"Sometimes great people make great mistakes."** Apostle Paul said, "Follow me **as** I follow Christ" (1 Corinthians 11:1).

In Acts chapter 17, Paul commended the people of Berea because they searched the scriptures diligently to see if his teachings were scripturally sound. **He said, "These were more noble than those in Thessalonica, in that they received the Word with all readiness, and searched the scriptures daily, whether those things were so" (Acts 17:11).**

When people, great people—preachers, pastors, public officials, politicians, friends, or whoever—when they start teaching things or doing things that prove to be erroneous or that contradict or are in conflict with the Word of God, that's when we know that person is walking in error, and we cannot agree with them, or we can't "follow" them in that teaching or in whatever it is.

I remember one time, I was driving along and listening to a nationally syndicated Christian radio broadcast program, and this minister, a "doctor," was conducting a call-in "Q and A" session. **Well, someone called in and asked him, "Is tithing for today?"**

He answered, "No," that tithing was an "Old Testament principle that was practiced under the Law and is not for today." He further stated that "tithing" was not mentioned in the New Testament." **Needless to say, upon hearing that, I almost lost control of my car.**

I don't know where that "doctor" got his credentials from, but he obviously did not study the Bible very well. In Matthew 23:23, Jesus addressed tithing. Jesus said,

> Woe unto you, scribes and Pharisees, hypocrites! For you pay tithe of mint and anise and cumin, and have omitted the weightier matters of the Law, judgment, mercy and faith: These ought you to have done, and not to leave the other undone.

Jesus did not say, "You ought not to tithe." He said along with "judgment, mercy and faith," you "ought not to leave the other [or the tithes] undone."

The writer of the book of Hebrews said in Hebrews 7:5,

> And verily they that are of the sons of Levi, **who receive the office of the priesthood, have a commandment to take tithes of the people** according to the Law, that is, of their brethren, though they come out of the loins of Abraham.

Those are New Testament Scriptures. That verifies to us now that tithing is addressed in the New Testament as well as the Old Testament. Jesus said we should not leave it "undone," and the writer of Hebrews affirms tithing as a New Testament doctrine.

If one would do a biblical study of tithing, they would discover that tithing is a profound concept or principle that was started in the Old Testament long before Moses came along with "the Law" and was affirmed and continued by Jesus Christ under the New Testament and grace.

In Genesis 14:18–20, **Abraham gave tithes to King Melchizedek** because he recognized the divine nature and the divine attributes of King Melchizedek (See also Hebrews 7:1–8). **In Genesis 28:22, Jacob promised to give God a tenth** of all that God had blessed him with because he recognized the importance of the "tenth part," which belongs to God.

The principle of tithing was so profound that God commanded it to be continued under the Law, and Jesus said it should not be left "undone" even under "grace"

in the New Testament. So I don't know what the "doctor" had been studying, but he clearly had not studied the tithe truthfully or objectively. **That's why we should not follow people blindly. Follow the Word of God.** Again, Paul said, "Follow me as I follow Christ," and he instructed us to "study to show thyself approved unto God, a workman that needs not to be ashamed, rightly dividing the Word of truth" (2 Timothy 2:15).

Another example of great people or prominent people walking in error comes from a nationally and internationally known minister who was the writer of several books. Up until his death a few years ago, this man was highly respected by the Christian church as a highly "anointed man of God" with a gift of prophecy.

In one of his books, he made several "predictions" about the year AD 2000. **Some of his predictions came true, but several did not,** such as, "Time would run out by 2000 AD," or that "Jerusalem would become the greatest and richest city on earth before 2000 AD."

Neither of those things happened, and there were other "missed" predictions in the book. This is a reminder that **"sometimes great people make great mistakes."** Beware of following people or being misled by people. Remember, **Apostle Paul said, "Follow me as I follow Christ."**

In the book of Acts, chapter 18, there was "a certain Jew named Apollos, an eloquent man and mighty in the Scriptures." The Bible says he was "instructed in the way of the Lord" and was "fervent in the Spirit." Although he was "instructed in the way of the Lord" and was "fervent in the Spirit," **Apollos still had an error in his preaching.** The Bible says he knew "only the baptism of John."

Thank God Aquila and his wife, Priscilla, knew the truth, and when they heard Apollos preach, **the Bible says they took him under their wings "and expounded unto him the way of God more perfectly" (Acts 18:26).** If we learn error or if we are taught error, then we will teach error, or we will preach error. We have a duty to share with one another, teach one another, and learn from one another so that we may be perfected in the way of the Lord (Galatians 6:6).

A few years ago, a very prominent and internationally known evangelist and pastor decided to run for the presidency of the United States of America. He spoke very eloquently about what he thought that God wanted him to do. So in order to prevent a conflict of interest ("separation of church and state"), **he announced that he would lay aside his ministry work and run for the presidency.** He campaigned for a while but did not make it through "the primaries." **Needless to say, he fell far short of becoming the president of the USA.**

In America, any US citizen has the right to run for any office that they are qualified for, but this pastor-evangelist felt very strongly about running for the presidency and must have forgotten that he already had the highest office in the land, that of a **"called"** minister of God. **As ministers of the gospel, we must be very careful about what we do with secular or political activities.**

Of course, that does not mean that we cannot be involved in secular or political activities, maybe even

hold political offices. In fact, we need Christians involved in politics, but we must be very, very careful. Apostle Paul said, "No man that warreth entangles himself with the affairs of this life; that he may please Him who has chosen him to be a soldier" (2 Timothy 2:4).

However, even a minister or "prophet" can be "presumptuous" and speak a "vision" or a desire out of his or her "own heart" or out of his or her own understanding. God said to Jeremiah, "They speak a vision of their own heart, and not out of the mouth of the Lord" (Jeremiah 23:16c). We must learn to "discern" the difference so that we are not misled.

Unfortunately, some folks who say they are "ministers" are not "called" into the ministry. Of course, there are different "callings" in the body of Christ. **The initial "call" is the call to salvation** when Jesus Christ calls us to be part of His Church, the **"the *Ekklesia*" or the "called out ones."** He "calls us out of darkness and into His marvelous light" (1 Peter 2:9b). **But then after salvation, there is a higher call, a "call to preach" or to minister the Word of God** to the people. The writer of the book of Hebrews said, "No man taketh this honor unto himself, but he that is called of God, as was Aaron" (Hebrews 5:4).

It does not matter how eloquent or prolific you are. Being eloquent or prolific or having great speaking ability does not make a person a "called" minister of the Gospel. **In fact, being eloquent or prolific can give rise to "false prophets" or people who say they are "ministers," but they are not "called,"** and because they are so eloquent and may have a lot of what we call "charisma," they are able to mislead a lot of people. **God said to Jeremiah, "I have not sent these prophets, yet they ran: I have not spoken to them, yet they prophesied" (Jeremiah 23:21).**

Chapter 5

Use Sound Hermeneutics

Sometimes we are subject to error because we have received bad or erroneous teaching. Erroneous teaching is prevalent throughout the Christian church, not to mention the "world" and secular institutions, **but errors in the Christian church should be corrected and kept to a minimum.**

Within the Christian church, we have doctrinal differences, denominational differences, and "personal" differences. Denominations, which denotes a division of the church, in and of themselves sometimes pass along bad doctrine or error.

Every "denomination" has taken a position or a "doctrine," which causes it to differ from some other denomination. They cannot all be right. Some of these "doctrines" are simply errors or bad teachings, but they are sometimes passed along and taught as "sound doctrines" of the Bible.

I am not saying that denominations are necessarily bad or that we don't necessarily need denominations, at least for the sake of order, **but there should not be so many doctrinal differences in the body of Christ (the Church).**

Every denomination that I am aware of uses some type of **"Holy Bible." Think about that!** If we interpret the Bible properly "by the Spirit" and "rightly divide" it, **the Bible should unite us and bring us together on "one accord," not divide us.** The reason why we have so much bad doctrine and erroneous teaching is that people are not using sound hermeneutics.

Hermeneutics is simply the practice and method by which we study and interpret scripture. In his book entitled *Hermeneutics*, **Bernard Ramm, defined *hermeneutics* as "that theological discipline which takes as its goal the proper interpretation of Scripture."** The Bible calls it **"rightly dividing the Word of truth"** (2 Timothy 2:15). If we use sound hermeneutics and "rightly divide" scripture, we will minimize and eliminate a lot of erroneous teachings and erroneous doctrines.

A few years ago, when I was president of the Baptist Ministers' Union of Macon, Georgia, I designed a Bible study to help ministers properly interpret Scripture. In the material, **I outlined five simple rules, which I called the "Rules of Hermeneutics."** I'd like to share them with you.

Five basic rules of hermeneutics

1. Remember, all Scripture is "inspired by God" (2 Timothy 3:16).
2. Be objective and strive to "rightly divide the Word of truth" (2 Timothy 2:15).

3. Keep Scripture "line upon line, precept upon precept, here a little, there a little" (Isaiah 28:9–10). In other words, make sure the Scriptures you are studying or comparing are in the same context or that they are dealing with the same subject matter.
4. Remember, the Spirit and the Word must always "bear record." The Spirit must always agree with the Word (1 John 5:7).
5. Remember, Scripture never contradicts Scripture. Therefore a "revelation" of the Scripture will never contradict other Scripture dealing with the same matter.

In addition to those five rules, we should use proper **exegesis** when studying the Bible. **According to Ramm, "Exegesis deals concretely with the text."** In other words, **when seeking to interpret Scripture, you exegete the text by reading out of the text exactly what is written.** Avoid **eisegesis** or reading something into the text that is not literally in the text or in any other Scriptures dealing with the same subject.

If we use "exegesis" and apply those five simple rules when studying and trying to interpret Scripture, we will make far fewer mistakes, and we will be more assured of a correct interpretation of God's Word.

Seminary and theological studies

It is also a good thing if a minister can attend seminary or take some theological courses to aid them in their personal growth, **but beware! Before you attend seminary or take theological courses, you need to be already very familiar with your Bible**. A seminary instructor may teach based on a particular bias that was based on their denomination or the unique teaching of that particular school or simply just that instructor's personal view. **Students, beware!**

I remember in one of the seminaries I attended, the instructor said something like, "Jesus was a Black man." Well, that got my attention right away. I happened to know my Bible well enough to know that Jesus's earthly father, **Joseph, was a Jew, born of the lineage of David and Abraham, who were Jews (Matthew 1:1–16).**

I also knew that the Jews descended from Shem, one of the sons of Noah and that the African/Ethiopian Black man descended from Ham, a different son of Noah (Genesis 10:1–8). **Ham gave birth to Cush, who was the African/Ethiopian Black man, but Joseph's lineage can be traced all the way back to Shem, who was the forefather of the Jews.** Needless to say, I did not accept the teaching that Jesus was a Black man because I was familiar with the Scriptures. **Students beware! Know your Bible!**

If you're going to use "sound hermeneutics" and "rightly divide" Scripture, **you've got to have a "Holy Bible"** that you can rely on as the Holy Word of God. **Remember, "all Scripture is inspired by God," but all "Bibles" are not inspired by God.** There are some Bibles that were written to change or undermine the original scriptural text, and some Bibles were written to undermine or deny the deity of Jesus Christ.

Whatever Bible you choose to rely on as the Word of God, be familiar with its background, how it came into print, and whether it was written to be true to the original Hebrew, Greek, and Aramaic text. **I personally use the King James Version Bible (KJV) or the New King James Version Bible (NKJV)** because I know how we got the King James Version Bible, and I believe the KJV Bible can be trusted as being accurate and true to the original text.

In response to instructions from King James, **when you have fifty-four to fifty-six Bible scholars and theologians agreeing on the best English word for translation out of the original Hebrew, Greek, or Aramaic text, then I believe that product (the KJV) can be trusted.**

There is a reason why some writings, which sounded like Scripture, were omitted from the Christian Holy Bible. They just didn't pass the Scripture test or the "canon" of the Holy Bible. They had to be tested and proven to be "inspired by God" by being compared to other known genuine Scripture, etc. before they were included in the "Holy Bible."

There are a number of writings, both during Old Testament times and New Testament times, which are not included in the Holy Bible that is used by Protestant Christians. **These books are called "the Apocrypha" or the "lost books" because they could not be authenticated** or because they simply contradicted or conflicted with known and verifiable Scripture; thus, they were not included in the books of the Holy Bible that is used by most Protestant Christians.

So get yourself a good "Holy Bible" that you can trust, and using "sound hermeneutics," you can identify, minimize, and eliminate erroneous doctrines or erroneous interpretations of the Holy Scriptures.

"Born of the water"

When it comes to using "sound hermeneutics," it's easy for any of us to violate the "rules of hermeneutics," especially when dealing with tradition, denominational doctrine, or something that is commonly said or taught. Recently, when reading about the late great Smith Wigglesworth, I was surprised to see that **in one of his sermons, he referred to being "born of water" (John 3:5) as water baptism.** I know probably most folks have been taught that in our churches, and it has been passed on from generation to generation, but it is erroneous teaching. Even the great Smith Wigglesworth fell victim to it.

If you take a closer look at the conversation between Jesus and Nicodemus in John chapter 3, you will see that the conversation is about two births, natural birth and spiritual birth. In response to Jesus's statement, "Except a man be born again he cannot see the kingdom of God," Nicodemus asked, "Can he enter a second time into his mother's womb, and be born?" (John 3:4).

Jesus answered Nicodemus, "Except a man be born of water and of the Spirit, he cannot enter into the kingdom of God." **This conversation is clearly about two births, "born of water" (natural birth) and born "of the Spirit" (spiritual birth).** This is made even clearer by what Jesus said in verse 6, **"That which is born of the flesh is flesh: and that which is born of the Spirit is spirit."** This misinterpretation of Scripture can happen to any of us for various reasons. We must be "vigilant" and diligent at "rightly dividing the Word of truth."

The rapture

Another biblical truth that is misunderstood because of bad hermeneutics is the doctrine of the **rapture of the church.** While the word "rapture" is not stated verbatim in the Bible, the event that "rapture" refers to is clearly stated in the Scriptures. It's sort of like the word **"Trinity,"** which is not actually stated in the Scriptures but references to God as a triune God and references to the triunity of the Godhead are found throughout the Scriptures (Matthew 28:19, Philippians 2:5–11, Colossians 2:8–10, just to name a few).

The event that is referred to as the "**rapture"** is deeply rooted and grounded in the Scriptures. First Thessalonians clearly says that when the trumpet sounds and the Lord returns, we shall be **"caught up [the Greek word is *harpazo*, which means "to seize or catch away"]** together with them in the clouds, to meet the Lord in the air" (I Thessalonians 4:13–18).

Unfortunately, because of bad hermeneutics, there is a lot of erroneous teaching on the rapture and when we should expect it to happen. Some teach "pretrib" (pre-tribulation) rapture, some "midtrib" rapture, and others teach a "posttrib" rapture. **Many Bible scholars, theolo-**

gians, and ministers teach that the rapture takes place in Revelation 4:1 when Jesus said to John, **"Come up hither,** and I will show thee things which must be hereafter."

Although I have heard all kinds of explanations and justifications, Revelation 4:1 cannot be the rapture or the "catching away" of the church. Jesus simply wanted John to come up "hither" or higher so that He could show him things "which must be hereafter." **A big tip-off is that it is not the "last" trumpet.**

Apostle Paul said we shall be "raised incorruptible" and "changed" at the "last trump" (1 Corinthians 15:51–52). The phrase **"last trump"** was used in the original text, so it was not a word that was added or inserted later to clarify the text, etc.

Following sound hermeneutics, the **"last"** trumpet does not sound until **Revelation 10:7 and Revelation 11:15.** This is the **"last"** trumpet that is mentioned in the Bible, and it looks like we (the "Church") are going to be around for at least part of the tribulation. **Fortunately, we will be gone when the "wrath of God" is poured out in Revelation chapters 15, 16, and 17. Please take a look at those chapters in your Bible.**

Chapter 6

Beware of Politics and Political Agendas

Two of the greatest problems that we have in America today are **politics and racism.** Our national, state, and local politics have devolved to a point where our major political parties are no longer working for the best interest of our nation. Our congressional people, our politicians, and our nation are deeply entrenched in **"partisan politics."** You would think that if our political parties (Democrats, Republicans, Libertarians, Independents, etc.) were truly working in the best interest of the nation, they would find several common areas of agreement. Nothing could be further from the truth.

The US Congress refuses to work together for the good of the nation (the people). **Sometimes the problem is philosophical or ideological in nature, or sometimes it's just plain old "politics."** Whatever the reason, our politicians refuse to see the same things. It's as if people are just blind and can't see.

As I am writing this book, our nation—and indeed, the whole world—is dealing with the **"coronavirus pandemic."** Doctors, scientists, and epidemiologists are providing certain scientific and medical facts to aid the nation in fighting and overcoming the virus, but for what looks like purely political reasons, some folks are resistant to the facts. **They simply insist on going along with their political group or their political agendas.** They go about manufacturing their own "facts" and are putting the nation and people's lives at serious risk while prolonging a national crisis, all for political reasons.

Someone has said, "You have a right to your own opinion but you don't have a right to your own facts." **Facts are just facts!** Facts are rooted and grounded in the truth. **"Facts" and "truths" are the same for everybody.** This is the same problem we have when sharing the gospel. Apostle Paul said,

> **But if our gospel be hid, it is hid to them that are lost:** In whom the god of this world has blinded the minds of them that believe not, lest the light of the glorious Gospel of Jesus Christ, who is the image of God, should shine unto them. (2 Corinthians 4:3–4)

The devil, working through politics, will blind you.

Nowadays, people place more emphasis on political agendas and being **"politically correct"** than they do on facts and truths and working for the good of the nation.

Politicians, political surrogates, and political pundits will **"spin"** the facts to benefit their agendas.

Even national and international TV news stations will sometimes **"cherry-pick"** the facts and put a **"slant" on news stories** because they may have a hidden agenda. We have to be very careful how we receive, process, and act on information unless it is from a trusted and reliable source. **Hypocrisy** is so apparent that **"partisan politics"** have made a lot of sources unreliable. **Beware of the evils of politics and those with political agendas.**

I'm not saying that we should not be involved in politics, but I am saying we must be very, very careful what we get involved in, whom we support, and how we deal with "facts" and "truths." **We must be careful not to become cynical or "sick" in our thinking** to the point that we refuse to accept facts and cannot be fair and objective when evaluating a situation or another individual for that matter.

When riding around in my car, I like listening to conservative Christian radio programs with preaching, teaching, and discussions on different topics. **These radio programs used to be reliable for honest discussions, facts, and truths** related to current concerns, but I've noticed over the years that some of them have become more and more partisan in how they view or discuss subject matter.

One day, while I was riding around listening to one of my favorite Christian radio stations that carries preaching, teaching, talk/discussions, and people calling in with comments or questions, I noticed that **the "talk" was so politically biased that it seemed they had become a "PAC"**

(political action committee) for a specific political party. So I switched the dial to another similar Christian radio station. **The same thing was going on.**

The "Christian" radio talk show hosts were presenting their "facts" and views in a biased manner to favor the political party that they obviously had chosen for themselves. It was both **sad** and **disgusting** to me. It was as if they were blind and simply could not see how to be objective. They were **"cherry-picking" the facts** and applying a **double standard** just to favor a political view or a political party. They must have been conscious of their ratings because they were obviously playing to their base. **They were unwittingly (or wittingly) contributing to one of the evils that is keeping our nation divided.**

Even prominent pastors, devoted church members, and well-respected spiritual leaders are being adversely affected by the politics of our day. **Sometimes it appears that they are brainwashed** and simply cannot see past the lies, deception, unethical, and sometimes unlawful tactics of politicians that they favor.

Some pastors are preaching partisan politics, even from the pulpit. They have lost the ability to be objective and preach "truth" while standing up for what is right ("righteousness"). Quite often, the unethical and ungodly acts are **so obvious that it is absolutely appalling** when pastors, ministers of the gospel, and "church folks" go along with it or actually endorse the behavior.

This "brainwashing" is not limited to supporters of any particular political party. I see it happening with supporters of both major political parties, Republicans and

Democrats. I listen to some of the prominent pastors and spiritual leaders of our nation, and it looks like **some of them have become so focused on a political agenda that they have become blind** to the "truth" and cannot tell the difference between right and wrong. I have begun to switch them off.

I am convinced that people sometimes see what they want to see. It does not matter how much documented facts or "hard" evidence is presented on an issue; **if it's not what some people want or what they're are looking for; they're simply not going to see it or accept the facts.** They will go on living in denial, believing what they want to believe. **It's like that old saying: "You can't see the forest for looking at the trees."**

No wonder church members are being deceived and misled because the church leaders are being deceived and misled. **Jesus said, "Can the blind lead the blind? Shall they not both fall into the ditch?" (Luke 6:39).** This is a great evil that is permeating the Church, and we need to be delivered from it. **It's as if people are "drinking the Kool-Aid" or the poisoned "tea" similar to the followers of Jim Jones** when they followed him blindly to their murder-suicide in Jonestown, Guyana, in 1978. **Wake up, Church! Wake up, Christians! Wake up, people!**

I consider myself a "conservative evangelical Christian," but I don't need preachers, Christian radio talk show hosts, and spiritual leaders giving me "half-truths" and "twisted facts" designed to conform to a political agenda while refusing to rebuke or correct the lies, deception, and even profanity being used by party leaders and those seeking political office. **Even the so-called "Christian" radio talk show hosts are simply catering to what they believe is their "base."**

On another occasion, during the presidential election campaign of 2020, the president of the United States, in order to stir up his supporters, used profanity-laced speech and told the crowd that if a group of fire truck operators who were spraying water on them to cool them off, **"If they are the enemy, take care of the SOBs" He didn't use the initials.** He used the actual words of the profanity.

I listened the next day to see if the Christian radio talk show hosts would rebuke that type of behavior, or at least put in a "disclaimer" to distance themselves from it. They are very knowledgeable and very well informed. They seem to stay up with the latest "talk" of the day, but on this and other unchristian and ungodly behavior by an individual, who is the standard bearer for the party and seemingly for the evangelical community, **"crickets." Not a word was said.**

We don't need Christian leaders and Christian radio talk show hosts giving us partisan political views. **We need pure, objective facts so that we can make good objective decisions for the good of the nation, the people that we serve, and perhaps even our own good.** Needless to say, in disgust, I switched the dial again and **turned to a "gospel station"** that mostly plays gospel music all day. That was soothing, and I felt safe for the moment.

The US Supreme Court

Even our US Supreme Court, the highest court in the land, is not immune to politics and the forces that can influence all of us. For whatever reason, sometimes those nine Supreme Court justices just get it wrong, such as the **"Dred Scott decision"** of 1857, which ruled that the US Constitution was not meant to include African Americans.

In more modern times, there have been other Supreme Court decisions that left me shaking my head in wonder. **You would think that out of nine Supreme Court justices, a majority of them would get it right when a decision has to be made at their level.** They are people who are professionals, well trained, accomplished lawyers and constitutional scholars, but they sometimes get it wrong. They too are heavily influenced and **sometimes persuaded by the politics of the day to be "politically correct"** in their decisions or to favor one side or the other in spite of not having a truly legal or constitutional basis for some of their decisions.

Again, while I was writing this book, sadly, one of the nine Supreme Court justices, **Judge Ruth Bader Ginsburg (aka "RBG") passed.** I'm sure that even as you read this, you will remember the firestorm that immediately erupted in the US Congress due to her passing. She was an acknowledged liberal judge, and the same day that she passed, probably while her body was still warm, both sides of Congress (Democrats and Republicans) began jockeying and maneuvering for an advantage to nominate her replacement on the US Supreme Court.

Senators who had publicly taken certain positions to block presidential nominations during a president's "lame duck" year, then all of a sudden flip-flopped and changed positions. **The hypocrisy was obvious.** It was well documented, and it was appalling.

As I said earlier, **I am a "conservative evangelical Christian,"** and I desire to have conservative judges but not at all cost. **We are not to go to the extreme of lying and deceiving and being hypocritical to obtain our goals, no matter how "right" we think they are.** It's as if we have forgotten that our God is in control, and if we simply do our part and do the right thing, He can and will work it out.

We have come to a time that the prophet Isaiah warned us about, when people would "call evil good and good evil" (Isaiah 5:20). Even when facts and circumstances are clear, it appears that we have difficulty judging matters fairly and objectively, **but the prophet Micah told us what God requires of us:** "He has shown thee, O man, what is good; and what does the Lord require of thee, but to do justly, and to love mercy, and to walk humbly with thy God?" (Micah 6:8).

Chapter 7

Beware of Racism

Racism also is one of the evils that is tearing our nation apart and keeping us divided as a nation. Racism is deeply embedded in our American culture, and it's not planning to go anywhere. Even 150 years after fighting a Civil War and fifty-seven years after Dr. Martin Luther King Jr. shared his **"dream"** with a nation engaged in a fight over Civil Rights, the evils of racism, racial discrimination, and racial hatred are still prevalent in America.

Even in this twenty-first century, we still have people who are fighting to maintain the ideals and the memorials of a war that was fought to keep another man enslaved, all because of the color of his skin. No American should be proud of that part of our nation's history, but it is history, and we cannot change it. Although we cannot change it, we should not be proud of it, and we should acknowledge that slavery was an evil part of our nation's history, and racism is an evil that we need to be delivered from. We have racism in some form or another (individual or systemic) in just about every aspect of American society, to include the justice system and especially law enforcement with police brutality, etc.

When I see the hypocrisy of conservative "right wing" Christians, I can understand how slavery and racism were allowed to thrive throughout our nation's history, even up to the present time, in spite of all those "Christians" and evangelical preachers who were supposedly "preaching the Bible." Not enough of them ("church folks") were willing to take a stand against racism and racial injustices.

Unfortunately, White folks aren't the only ones who are perpetuating racism. Being racially prejudiced is not limited to any particular race or color. We have a lot of Black folks (and I'm sure there are some Red, Yellow, and Brown ones too) who are racially prejudiced.

Dr. King's "dream" of an America where every human being is treated justly and fairly, without discrimination because of their race or the color of their skin, is a dream that it appears that most Americans ascribe to but don't practice or strive toward. Around January 15 of every year, I assist with leading a "MLK Jr. March" in commemoration of the life of the late reverend Dr. Martin Luther King Jr. Hundreds and hundreds of people (mostly Black) march with us, but thank God some of my White friends and some that I do not know march with us. They are trying to help us fulfill the dream that **Dr. King had of a "beloved community." However, after "the march," most of my Black friends, ministers and pastors included, go back "to business as usual."**

This is especially noticeable during local, state, and even national elections. Most Black folks expect other

Black folks to vote for the "Black candidate," primarily because of the color of their skin. It does not matter what their qualifying factors are or the "disqualifying factors." **If you are a Black person, you are expected to "vote Black." Whatever happened to "the dream"?**

Voting by ethnicity or skin color happens across the aisle with our White brothers and sisters as well. If there is a close political contest, **the political candidate will invariably "play the race card"** to try to gain an advantage. This happens on both sides of the ethnic aisle, but it is a sad commentary on all of us that in America today, we still resort to voting by race.

Our ministers, pastors, church leaders, and church members are not doing enough to overcome this scourge on society. I meet with and am a member of several local ministerial alliances, some predominantly Black and some mixed (Thank God). I see firsthand the lackadaisical attitude when it comes to race relations, and **I see ministers and other folks who simply want to maintain the status quo of "us versus them."** They say they believe in "the dream," but they're not doing anything to practice the principles of "the dream" or to achieve the fulfillment of it.

In a recent street protest over the killing of a Black man by police, one group of "White supremacist" protesters were demonstrating their hatred for the Jewish people, shouting, "The Jews will not replace us." **The Jews are another ethnic group who has been discriminated against simply because of their nationality or ethnicity,** perhaps because they are identified in the Bible as "God's chosen people."

We ought to love every human being and treat everybody right, but we'd better make sure that we don't have any jealousy or hatred toward the Jews or any other people for that matter. **Concerning the Jewish people, God said to Abraham, "I will bless them that bless thee, and curse him that curseth thee: and in thee shall all the families of the earth be blessed" (Genesis 12:3).** God chose to bless all of us through the Jewish people, so why the hatred?

We are all subject to prejudices and biases, including racial prejudices, but **we must become racially sensitive and consciously resist the temptation to follow our natural inclinations to judge a person or treat a person differently simply because of the "color of their skin" or their ethnicity or nationality.** Failure to do this is one of the evils that is devouring our nation and keeping the nation, including "church folks," divided.

As a nation, we need to work harder at "racial reconciliation." We need to work untiringly to fulfill the "dream" and **achieve the "beloved community"** that was envisioned by Dr. Martin Luther King Jr. **The "beloved community" is simply a rephrasing of a commandment given to us by Jesus Christ:**

> **A new commandment I give unto you, that you love one another; as I have loved you, that you love one another.** By this shall all men know that you are My disciples, if you have love one to another. (John 13:34–35)

Chapter 8

The Attack on the Church

In chapter 1, I said, "The first thing you want to do in order to be delivered from the evil is to recognize the presence and the cause of evil." The devil, or satan, is the root cause of most of the evil that we encounter. **He is particularly attacking God's Church,** trying to afflict her, trying to deceive her, trying to divide her, trying to destroy her, and trying to stop her from accomplishing her mission.

Jesus Christ knew that the Church would have a formidable and powerful **spiritual "adversary" by the name of satan.** That's what the name **"satan"** means in Hebrew, **"adversary."** So when Jesus said, "Upon this rock I will build My Church," He established the "Church" upon Himself (the "Rock," the revelation of the truth that He is the Son of God) **and declared that "the gates of hell shall not prevail against it" (Matthew 16:18).**

Please don't be offended when I refer to the Church as "it" or "she" or "her" because as an organization, the Church may be referred to as "it," **but the Church is more than just an organization**. She is also a living organism of

living, breathing human beings who have been "called out of darkness and into His marvelous light" (1 Peter 2:9). Therefore, I may use those terms interchangeably, so please don't be offended, **but in general, a "church" is "an organized body of baptized believers" and followers of Jesus Christ.**

We also understand that **the word "church" has a twofold meaning.** *Church* not only refers to the people, but the word "church" is also used to refer to the building designated for the people to gather for worship and other religious activities **(the "church house").** You should be able to determine the appropriate meaning by the context of the passage in which the word is used.

The Greek word for "church" is *ekklesia*, which means "the called out ones." When Jesus said, "Upon this rock I will build My **Church**" (Matthew 16:18), He was talking about the **"called out ones,"** so He established His Church, equipped her and **gave her access to supernatural power.**

> **But you shall receive power after that the Holy Ghost is come upon you:** and shall be witnesses unto Me both in Jerusalem, and in all Judea, and in Samaria, and unto the uttermost part of the earth. (Acts 1:8)

The "Church" is made up of people who have been "called out" of a world of sin. In other words, the "members of the Church" are those who have **"accepted" Jesus Christ** as their Lord and Savior and are committed to following Him. Jesus Christ calls this acknowledgement and acceptance of Him a spiritual experience and a phenomenon, which He calls being **"born again."** He says in **John 3:3, "Except a man be born again he cannot see the kingdom of God."** This spiritual experience causes the "Church member" to be a candidate to receive the supernatural power mentioned above in Acts 1:8.

The fact that the Church has access to supernatural power (the Holy Ghost) does not stop the Church from being attacked by the devil. **Peter told us in 1 Peter 5:7, "Be sober, be vigilant; because your adversary the devil, as a roaring lion, walketh about, seeking whom he may devour."**

Our adversary the devil is attacking the very pillars of our faith. He has sown so many lies and "half-truths" and errors into the Church that **it's difficult nowadays to distinguish between the Church and "the world."** Make no mistake about it, satan is behind the lies and erroneous doctrines that are so prevalent in many of our churches today. Jesus said the devil was a "liar from the beginning and the father of lies" (John 8:44).

First of all, the Church is not supposed to be like "the world." Jesus prayed to the Father in the seventeenth chapter of John, "They are not of the world, even as I am not of the world. Sanctify them through Thy truth: Thy Word is truth" (John 17:16–17). I'm not saying that we should be judgmental, but we are supposed to be different from "the world." **Peter said,**

> **But you are a chosen generation, a royal priesthood, a holy nation, a peculiar**

> **people;** that you should show forth the praises of Him who has called you out of darkness into His marvelous light. (1 Peter 2:9)

We have too many church folks, church members, and even ministers of the gospel who are trying to be just like the world. They dress like the world. They act like the world, and they look like the world. You know the saying "if it looks like a duck, walks like a duck, and quacks like a duck"—you know the rest of the story.

I know we say, "It's not about the clothes, it's about the heart," but that's only part true. There is another saying we need to think about: **"Anything that's holy on the inside, it will show up on the outside."** We need to think about that and be who we are in Christ even if it affects how we dress and how we act (which it should).

Secondly, some of our churches are going too far trying to attract people, especially trying to attract the young people or the "millennials" of today's generation. I understand the need to be creative and try to present the ministry in a way that our youths can relate, but we should be careful not to go too far.

A few years ago, there was **an effort by some churches to set up a "nightclub" atmosphere in the church. This was an attempt to draw young people** by replicating a **"nightclub"** to socialize them and get them used to a nightclub atmosphere. I'm glad that idea didn't last long, or at least I hope it didn't.

The "church house" has to be different from a "club-house" or a nightclub. The atmosphere in the "church house" should be different, holy, reverent. **The lighting in the "church" should not be dark or dim, like a night-club**, unless for whatever reason, it just can't be helped or it serves a special purpose for a particular occasion.

Generally speaking, the church should be well lit so that you can follow along in your Bible during worship services or Bible studies, etc. **People should not come to church to get a "nightclub" experience.** They should "come to church" to have a holy, reverential, **"worship experience"** with Almighty God.

People are trying to bring everything that's in the world into the Church and trying to get the Church to allow any-thing and accept everything that the world accepts. **The Church is supposed to be different from the world.** The Church is supposed to be **"the salt of the earth" and "the light of the world" (Matthew 5:13–14).** It looks like instead of the Church "changing" the world, the world is "changing" the Church.

We have folks who say they are "church folks," mem-bers of the church who will curse, swear, and use profanity without giving it a second thought or with little or no prov-ocation, just like other folks do. **Jesus said, "But let your communication be, Yea, yea: Nay, nay: for whatsoever is more than these cometh of evil" (Matthew 5:37).**

We have churches and folks who say they are **"mem-bers" of the Church,** who condone and engage in worldly, secular, and sometimes sinful activities: gambling, drink-ing, partying, fornicating, and "shacking up" instead of getting married, which God has ordered and ordained (Genesis 2:24, Hebrews 13:4). **It seems like the devil has blinded church members just like he has blinded people of the "world" so that we don't know right from wrong anymore, or we just don't care.**

God's hierarchy

When man sinned in the garden of Eden, God established a **hierarchy, an "order of authority,"** for the man and the woman. **God ordained that from that time on, the man would have the position of authority over the woman (Genesis 3:16).** This hierarchy is reestablished and reaffirmed throughout the Bible as **"sound doctrine"** for the Church (1 Corinthians 11:4; 1 Corinthians 14:34, 40; 1 Timothy 2:12).

In the Church, the ministerial "callings" and gifts have a hierarchy in order to prevent confusion in the Body of Christ. Apostle Paul tells us in the book of 1 Corinthians,

> Now are you the Body of Christ, and members in particular. And God has set some in the church, **first apostles, secondarily prophets, thirdly teachers**, then gifts of healings, helps, governments, diversities of tongues. (1 Corinthians 12:27–28)

After affirming the hierarchy for the church Paul said, **"Let all things be done decently and in order" (1**

Corinthians 14:40). There is not supposed to be any confusion in the church concerning positions of authority and where each member fits in.

I'm sorry, sisters, but God's hierarchy establishes that the man is supposed to occupy the highest position in the Church, such as the pastor or the overseer. This is not my opinion; it is in accordance with the "order of authority" as ordained by God and is maintained throughout the Scriptures, **both Old Testament and New Testament.**

In Numbers 27:16, Moses prayed unto God, saying, "Let the Lord, the God of all flesh set a man over the congregation." Apostle Paul recognized this hierarchy when he said, "But I suffer not a woman to teach or to usurp authority over the man, but to be in silence" (1 Timothy 2:12).

Surely, someone will say, "What about the prophetess Deborah? Didn't she rule as a judge over God's people?" Well, not taking anything away from Deborah, but if you look at the situation that she was involved in, you might see her in a slightly different light. **When Deborah judged Israel, the nation of Israel was in a backslidden state.** The Bible says that Israel again did evil in the sight of the Lord, "And the Lord sold them into the hand of Ja'bin, king of Canaan" (Judges 4:1–5).

Even as judge over Israel, Deborah did not have full or final authority over them because she wisely called for Barak and reminded him that God had delivered Sisera, their enemy, into his hands. **To which, Barak replied, "If thou will go with me, then I will go: but if thou will not**

go with me, then I will not go" (Judges 4:6–8). This lets us know that although Deborah was a judge, she did not have final authority over the affairs of Israel.

There are many other scriptures throughout the Bible that affirm "God's hierarchy" for order between the man and the woman, such as Isaiah 3:12 and 1 Corinthians 11:3. God gave clear instructions for His established hierarchy to minimize satan's being able to cause confusion in the Church over authority because human nature draws us toward positions of authority, and satan is able to exploit that natural tendency.

Pastors should counsel female ministers who have pastoral aspirations and make them aware of the Scriptures and biblical principles of God, which give guidance for every member of the body of Christ to follow. If God made you a man, then He expects you to honor and accept the scriptural guidance that pertains specifically to a man. **Likewise, if God made you a woman, He expects you to honor and accept the scriptural guidance that pertains specifically to a woman.** Otherwise, there is going to be a lot of confusion and disorder in the Body of Christ (the Church).

Don't worry. God knows who you are, and He knows why you were born male or female and what He has ordained you to do. His "callings" and His instructions are always in harmony with His Word. **First Corinthians 12:18 says, "But now has God set every member in the body, as it has pleased Him."** Second Timothy 2:13 says, "If we believe not, yet He abideth faithful: He cannot deny Himself." God knows where He has placed you in the Body, and He knows what He has ordained for you to do, **but He is not going to "deny" His own Word or do anything contrary to His Word.**

Of course, **women can and should be used to serve in the Church** and in various ministries of the Church, and they should be allowed to preach the gospel when they acknowledge "a call" from God for such a purpose. **Apostle Paul used women in ministry quite often**, and he recommended that the church in Rome "receive" them and "assist" them in whatever area they had need.

Apostle Paul said to the leadership of the church in Rome,

> I commend unto you Phebe our sister, which is a servant of the church which is at Cenchrea: **That you receive her in the Lord, as becometh saints, and that you assist her in whatever business she has need of you:** for she has been a succorer of many, and of myself also. (Romans 16:1–2)

Paul said Phebe was "a servant of the church." The word "servant" comes from the Greek word *diakoneos,* which is the same word from which we get our English word "deacon." In Romans chapter 16, Apostle Paul went on to acknowledge several women and men and asked the Roman church to receive them because they had assisted him and been very faithful in the work of the ministry (Romans 16:3–15).

Women ministers or **"prophetesses" (which are female prophets)**, are mentioned repeatedly in the Old Testament and New Testament Scriptures. Aaron's sister Miriam was a prophetess (Exodus 15:20), and we've already talked about Deborah the prophetess, who judged Israel during some difficult times (Judges 4:1–4).

When Jesus was born and was taken to the temple to be circumcised (on the eighth day), **there was a prophetess there by the name of Anna.** The Bible says,

> She did not depart from the temple, but served God with fastings and prayers night and day. And she coming in that instant gave thanks likewise unto the Lord, and spoke of Him to all them that looked for redemption in Jerusalem. (Luke 2:36–38)

In the book of Acts, chapter 21, **Phillip the Evangelist (one of the seven original deacons) had four daughters who had the gift of prophecy.** The Scriptures say, "And the same man had four daughters, virgins, which did prophesy" (Acts 21:8–9). So women have spiritual gifts and "callings" as well as men and should be allowed to serve in the church, but both women and men should recognize the "hierarchy" or order of authority that God has ordained for His Church.

Our ultimate goal should be to walk in God's "perfect will" and to "perfect" and "edify" the Body of Christ **(please see "The fivefold ministry" in this chapter and Ephesians 4:11).** We should strive to **"prove what is that**

good, and acceptable, and perfect, will of God" (Romans 12:2).

That is not to say that "we are perfect," but we are striving for the perfection and the maturity that God intends for us to have. Apostle Paul said,

> Brethren, I count not myself to have apprehended: but this one thing I do, forgetting those things that are behind, and reaching forth to those things that are before, **I press toward the mark of the prize of the high calling of God in Christ Jesus. (Philippians 3:13–14)**

We must "press toward the mark" by operating within the boundaries of the word that God has called us to preach.

In the early 1990s, after sitting down and talking with several of our "gifted" sisters, **I initiated a ministry for women called the Ministry of Inspired Sister Servants (MISS).** This ministry allowed more women to minister and serve in the church, and it effectively **enhanced our traditional ministries** that were already established.

After a few years, the female minister who had been selected and later elected to be over that ministry approached me and said **she felt "led" to initiate her own ministry to meet even more needs in the Body of Christ.** After consultation with her, I discovered that her "vision for her ministry" fit in well with the overall "vision" that I had for the church, **so we (the church) authorized her to establish "her" ministry** and become the founder and minister over it. **The ministry was called Turning Point Ministry Healing Clinic (no affiliation with David Jeremiah's "Turning Point").** The ministry was a blessing to our church and to the community at large.

I'm happy to say that she didn't go out and start her own church or ascribe to be the pastor over a church but worked within the authority of the organized church where she had been placed by God. **I'm saying all this to say that women (and men) can do all that God wants them to do within the boundaries and guidance that's given in the Scriptures.** It's simply a matter of letting God lead you to the "church" and to the pastor where He wants you to be and then submitting to their authority and leadership.

Marriage

God's hierarchy is to continue even in marriage. Marriage, between a man and a woman, has a special significance to God. **Marriage between a man and a woman symbolizes Jesus Christ's relationship to the Church**, which is the **"bride" of Christ.** "Therefore, as the Church is subject unto Christ, so let the wives be to their husbands in everything" (Ephesians 5:24).

This hierarchy that God has ordained is not demeaning or disrespectful to a person's human worth. **As human beings, regardless of gender, we are all equal before God, but someone has to have "the position of authority,"** so God has ordained a hierarchy, an order of authority, to minimize and eliminate confusion in marriage and in the

Body of Christ. **The topic of "marriage" will be revisited under "The Attack on the Family" (chapter 10).**

Gay or homosexual lifestyles

Some churches now accept the gay lifestyle as being an acceptable practice; consequently, they allow or even conduct gay marriages and license and ordain gay priests or gay ministers to lead their congregations. This is not only erroneous and bad doctrine, but it is **heresy, a complete departure from biblical teaching.** God condemns that kind of behavior in the Bible, just like He condemns certain heterosexual behaviors. **This topic also will be revisited under "The Attack on the Family" (chapter 10).**

In the Old Testament, homosexual relationships were condemned as **"an abomination" (Leviticus 18:22)**, and God still frowned upon it in the New Testament, calling it **"vile affections"** and "gave them over to **a reprobate mind" (Romans 1:26–28).** Just because something is "legal" in the courts does not mean that the Church should practice it or condone it. **Apostle Paul said in Romans 10:23, "All things are lawful for me, but all things are not expedient: all things are lawful for me, but all things edify not."** Just because something is "lawful" does not mean it will "edify" you or build you up.

Yes, we are to love everybody and treat everybody right, whether they are gay or "straight," but when the laws of man contradict the laws and principles of God as given to us in the Holy Bible, **Peter and the Apostles said, "We ought to obey God rather than men" (Acts 5:29).**

How did this happen in the Church? How did we get so far away from "sound" biblical doctrine in the Church? The book of Jude gives us the answer. Jude said we should

> earnestly contend for the faith that was once delivered unto the saints. For there are certain men, crept in unawares, who were before of old ordained to this condemnation, **ungodly men,** turning the grace of our God into lasciviousness, and denying the only Lord God, and our Lord Jesus Christ. (Jude verses 3–4)

People who were not "true believers" invaded the Church or "crept in unawares" while the Church's guard was down, and they influenced the Church and started erroneous doctrines or "ungodly" practices in the Church. Now some churches are blindly going along with the trend or whatever is "politically correct." **Please remember this: just because something is "legal" or "politically correct" or even popular does not mean that it is "edifying" or acceptable to God.**

Halloween

Make no mistake about it, the "Church" is constantly under attack. Our adversary, the devil, has been working against the Church in a myriad of ways, **sometimes overtly and sometimes covertly or in very subtle ways.** The devil has disguised his attacks so deceptively that sometimes, he is able to get the Church to willfully carry out his activities. **Halloween is one of those activities.**

Halloween is an activity that a lot of churches and "church folks" happily engage in. **I used to be one of those "church folks," but then I came into the knowledge of the truth, and I stopped celebrating that occasion.** It's just like Jesus said in John 8:31–32, "If you continue in My Word, then are you My disciples indeed; And you shall know the truth, and the truth shall make you free."

Some years ago, when encyclopedias were in full use, I did some research on Halloween. **Using *Encyclopedia Britannica*, I found out that Halloween was the "Celtic Festival of Samhain" and the "most favorable time for divination."** It was "the only time in which the help of the devil was invoked (for marriage, luck, health and death)."

***Encyclopedia Americana* informed me that Halloween "predates Christian times."** Several years before the coming of Christ, Celtic priests known as druids used October 31 **to honor their sun god and a satanic god known as "Samhain, lord of the dead."**

On the "satanic ritual calendar," they used to carry Halloween as the biggest celebration on the Satanists' calendar. Discovering these facts and truths about Halloween, I had to stop celebrating it. **I just cannot see how Halloween is an event that Christians should observe and celebrate.**

First Thessalonians 5:2 instructs us to "abstain from all appearance of evil." When you think about the devil costumes, monster masks, and skeletons of the dead, you can readily see the evil that's being portrayed ("just for fun"). Halloween not only promotes evil, but it is the devil's holiday.

Satan has disguised his holiday very well, and now you have Christians and churches and "church folks" who will fight you over that day, not knowing or not caring that the devil is behind it, and it is intended to celebrate evil.

Public prayer and Christian symbols

The laws that were passed to stop prayer in public schools and in other public settings were nothing but the overt work of satan. **Remember, "We don't wrestle against flesh and blood, but against principalities, against powers, against the rulers of the darkness of this world, against spiritual wickedness in high places" (Ephesians 6:12).**

I'm glad that when I was in elementary school and in high school (in the '60s), our school teachers did not adhere to that law. **Throughout my elementary and high school days in the public schools, we would start our days with prayer and "devotion."** That went a long ways in helping our families give us a strong foundation, upon which we could grow and build.

Now the attack has expanded and includes anything "Christian" or anything "Bible." Students are discouraged from bringing their Bibles to school by school officials. Teachers and employees of even private companies are prohibited from displaying their Bibles or Christian symbols on their desks or in their offices.

Cities across the United States are requiring that the Ten Commandments and other Christian or biblical symbols be removed from prominent public view. It's all a satanic attack upon the Christian faith and upon the Church to try to stop the Church or try to hinder Her from carrying out Her mission.

Church attendance and the coronavirus, etc.

With the coronavirus pandemic, satan is even trying to use the pandemic to try to stop or hinder church attendance or essential church activities. I'm not saying that satan caused it, but I'll bet if you could check it close enough, you may find that satan had a hand in it. When people have evil or nefarious intentions or make mistakes such that a virus of that magnitude gets loosed upon the population, **who do you think causes mistakes like that?**

So we have a coronavirus pandemic, affecting people and nations all over the world. People are wearing face masks, "socially distancing" themselves, and "sheltering at home," trying to take the necessary precautions, and rightfully so, but an interesting phenomenon is going on. **The devil is using the pandemic or taking advantage of it to put fear in people and discourage them from "going to church" or engaging in "in-house" and "in-person" church activities.**

People, including "church folks," are saying they are **"sheltering at home"** and are afraid to even go to church. **Due to the "pandemic," many of our churches have**

closed their doors for worship and other essential spiritual activities at the church.

During the pandemic, **"mega churches"** are at a disadvantage, except for media and online type of services, due to some state and local city governments are restricting the size of gatherings, and some even prohibit churches to open for worship services because of their large congregations.

The smaller and medium-sized churches can gather easier with "social distancing," **but churches must find a way for the house of God to be accessible for basic spiritual in-person and in-house services,** not recklessly or foolishly but prayerfully and wisely, following appropriate health and safety precautions.

If the governing bodies can figure out a way for private businesses and some public services to carry on safely, surely the Church can figure it out too. We are supposed to have the aid of the Holy Spirit to guide us, but Jesus did say in one parable, "The children of this world in their generation are wiser than the children of light" (Luke 16:8b).

I will acknowledge that this pandemic has made the Church better in some cases and wiser. **It has forced us to engage in "virtual" activities** and use the Internet and online technology more, but I would remind you that the **Internet and online services (YouTube, Facebook streaming, and Zooming) cannot replace in-person and in-house prayer and worship.**

All those technologies are excellent tools and should be used when practical, **but they cannot replace the fellowship that takes place when "the Church" gathers**

together, to worship together, at the house of God. In fact, the Church was designed to gather together as "one body in Christ" and receive nourishment together (1 Corinthians 12:12, Ephesians 4:16).

We are further directed in the book of Hebrews to, **"Forsake not the assembling of yourselves together,** as the manner of some is; but exhorting one another: and so much the more as you see the day approaching" (Hebrews 10:25).

The Body of Christ needs to assemble and gather together as "one body" and in "one place" regularly. In the book of Acts, they were able to do this even though they came under intense persecution. I understand that in some countries, some religions are forbidden, especially Christianity, **but even in those countries, Christians find a way to gather together, sometimes secretly in their own homes or in "underground" locations.**

Fortunately for us here in the United States, **because of the First Amendment to the US Constitution, we are not restricted or forbidden** to have religious gatherings, except in some rare instances, such as the coronavirus pandemic. **We must make sure that satan, through whatever means, doesn't use that to stop or weaken the Church.**

In September 2020, during the pandemic, **one mega church pastor on his regularly televised worship service gathered his church outside in the rain using umbrellas** while he preached to them from a well-improvised pulpit with a great sound system covered with plastic. I commend him for calling the congregation together to have worship and hear the Word, but I don't think I would've gone that far, especially with a spacious sanctuary just a few feet away. **Zeal is good, but we must also pray for wisdom and exercise godly wisdom along with our faith.**

Baptism

So we must be careful and not let the devil use the coronavirus pandemic to close the church doors and keep her from having the in-person or in-house worship and fellowship that she is instructed to have. We can preach, teach, meet, and use the Internet and online technologies, and **many churches are now receiving new members through those kind of services. Some even give communion through online services, but it's hard to do a baptism service online.** I haven't heard of that yet. There are some things we've got to do in-house or at least in person. **Let us exercise our faith in God and pray for godly wisdom on how to get it done safely and in a way that glorifies God.**

Baptism is an act that needs to be carried out literally in person and with an "authorized agent of the Church." **By definition, to "baptize" means to emerge or immerse in water.** The word **"baptize" or "baptism" comes from the Greek word *baptizo*, and it means "to make fully wet."** It literally means for someone to be physically "dunked or immersed underwater." For the most part, we Baptists believe in immersing you underwater when we baptize you. That's one doctrine I'm pretty sure we got right. Churches and pastors who are taking in church members through the Internet and through online services need to figure out some way to get them physically baptized using an "authorized agent of the Church."

That does not mean that baptism saves you. A person is "saved" when they "confess with their mouth and believe in their heart that God raised Jesus Christ from the dead" (Romans 10:9). **Otherwise, the thief on the cross would've had to come down from the cross and be baptized in order to "be with Jesus in paradise" (Luke 23:39–43).**

However, when a person is "saved," if they are physically able, they need to follow up their salvation with the public act of baptism by an authorized agent of the Church. **Mark 16:16 says, "He that believeth and is baptized shall be saved."** The Ethiopian eunuch said to Phillip in the book of Acts, **"See, here is water. What does hinder me to be baptized?" (Acts 8:36).**

Even Jesus, before He entered into ministry, went to John the Baptist and got baptized. The Bible says, "But John forbad Him, saying, I have need to be baptized by Thee, and comest Thou to me?" And Jesus, answering, said unto him, **"Suffer it to be so now: for thus it becometh us to fulfill all righteousness" (Matthew 3:14–15).** If Jesus Christ got baptized and told us to baptize, then we ought to make sure that we do it. In fact, it is part of our **"Great Commission."**

The Bible says in Matthew 28:18–20,

> And Jesus came and spoke unto them, saying, All power is given unto Me in heaven and in earth. **Go ye therefore and teach**

> **all nations, baptizing them in the name of the Father, and of the Son, and of the Holy Ghost:** Teaching them to observe all things whatsoever I have commanded you: and, lo, I am with you always, even unto the end of the world.

Christians all over the world call that our "Great Commission." That's what Jesus has called and "commissioned" us to do.

Church membership

Unless you're talking about "mega churches," it was difficult enough to get people to attend church (in the building) before the coronavirus pandemic. Now it's more difficult than ever. **I'm a firm believer that people ought to attend a local church regularly as directed by Hebrews 10:25 ("Forsake not the assembling of yourselves together"), "join" it, and become an "official member" of the congregation.**

Members of the "Body of Christ" ought to identify with the Body of Christ. Prior to the coronavirus pandemic, it was not unusual for me to meet people, talk to them, and after a little while see that we had a lot in common as "believers." They would be telling me about how good the Lord is and about everything that God had done for them, and **I'd ask them the million-dollar question: "Where's your church membership?" Or "Who's your pastor?"**

More often than not, the response would be, "I don't go to church," or "Well, I attend different churches," or "I don't have a pastor," or "I go there but I haven't joined. I'm not a member."

All those responses are problematic. They indicate that these "Christian believers" are not really in God's will for them. **God wants the members of His Body to be "pastored"** and have regular worship and fellowship together as "one body in Christ." **God said in Jeremiah 3:15, "I will give you pastors after My heart which shall feed you with knowledge and understanding."**

Members of the Body of Christ need to be accountable to a local church and accountable to a local pastor through membership in the Church. Oftentimes, Jesus referred to members of His Body as "sheep." Sheep need a "shepherd" (a pastor). They need to be fed, and they need to be led and orchestrated to accomplish the mission of the Church.

I remember one time, **I was attending a funeral**, and the person who was being buried evidently did not attend church very much, if at all. In an effort to comfort the family and friends, **the preacher said, "You know, you don't have to attend church to be saved and go to heaven."** Well, that is true, but people also need to know that churchgoing should follow salvation and **is an "act of faith,"** which is essential to the constant nourishment of the spirit and soul.

Being a friend of mine, I approached the preacher after the funeral and said, "That statement was not the whole truth, and it will not help us get people 'saved' and attending the church."

He chuckled and said, "They'll be coming back, Rev."

I certainly hope that he's right, but I still believe that while we're trying to give comfort and consolation, we ought to use funerals to give people the truth with as much love as we can. **If you really love the Lord, you ought to "join" His Church and assemble with the congregation as often as you can (Hebrews 10:25).**

The fivefold ministry

Something else that God provides through Church membership, church attendance, and church affiliation is the "perfecting of the Body of Christ." Ephesians 4:8 says, "When He (Jesus) ascended up on high, He led captivity captive, and gave gifts unto men." **The Scripture goes on to say, "And He gave some apostles, and some, prophets; and some, evangelists; and some, pastors and teachers, for the perfecting of the saints" (Ephesians 4:11).**

These five different kinds of ministerial gifts or "callings" are known as "the fivefold ministry." Their purpose is noted in the Scripture:

> **For the perfecting of the saints, for the work of the ministry, for the edifying of the Body of Christ;** Till we all come in the unity of the faith, and of the knowledge of the Son of God, unto a perfect man, unto

> the measure of the stature of the fullness of Christ. (Ephesians 4:12–13)

In other words, their purpose is to build us up (edify) and work on us until we look like Jesus Christ, until we be "perfected" in Christ.

Church members cannot grow and mature properly if they are not attending church regularly and receiving preaching, teaching, spiritual nourishment, and **instructions from an anointed minister of God.** Receiving constant preaching or teaching outside the Church from others who may not be "called" or who otherwise may be unqualified is dangerous to the individual, the Church, and to the community.

Chapter 9

The Attack on the Holy Bible

Not only is the Church under attack by the devil, but the Holy Bible also is under direct attack by the devil. Satan has launched a direct attack against the Holy Bible or against the Holy Word of God using people, organizations, and institutions, some wittingly and some unwittingly. **Remember Ephesians 6:12,**

> **For we wrestle not against flesh and blood, but against principalities, against powers, against the rulers of the darkness of this world, against spiritual wickedness in high places.**

There is a **subtle** and sometimes **overt** attack against the Bible as the Word of God. **I am convinced that's one of the reasons that we have so many "versions" of the Bible in print today.** Some of these "Bibles" simply cannot be trusted as the Word of God. That's why I said earlier, in chapter 5 ("Use Sound Hermeneutics"), **to choose a Bible that you can trust as the Holy Word of God.**

There are all kinds of Bibles available. **There are Bibles that were written to obviously detract from or to change the Word of God.** There are Bibles on the market today designed to **"neuter"** the Bible or to specifically change references to God in the masculine gender to a neutral or feminine gender. **Beware of Bibles that are guilty of that kind of distortion or mishandling of the Word of God.**

Some of these Bible publishers are simply "making a killing" from publishing all kinds of Bibles, for all kinds of people, some with ulterior motives. **I see Bibles now that has to be "updated" with "new editions"** every year like a high school or college textbook. **Excuse me! The Word of God does not need to be "updated" with "new editions" because the Word of God does not "change."**

God said in Malachi 3:6, "I am the Lord, I change not." The writer of the book of Hebrews said, "Wherein God, willing more abundantly to show unto the heirs of promise **the immutability of His counsel,** confirmed it by an oath" (Hebrews 6:17). **In other words, God gave His Word.** John 1:1 tells us, "In the beginning was the Word, and the Word was with God, and the Word was God." Then the writer of Hebrews proclaimed, **"Jesus Christ the same yesterday, and today, and forever" (Hebrews 13:8).**

God thinks very highly of His Word, and He reverences it and holds it in high esteem because **the Word of**

God was "inspired" or "breathed out" by God Himself. The psalmist said in Psalm 138:2,

> I will worship toward Thy holy temple, and praise Thy name for Thy loving kindness and for Thy truth: **for Thy has magnified Thy Word above all Thy name.**

Again, the psalmist said in Psalm 119:89, "Forever, O Lord, Thy Word is settled in heaven." We are supposed to "change" and conform to the Word of God, not "change" the Word because the Word of God is "immutable" and unchangeable. It is "settled" in heaven.

The book of Revelation says if any man "adds" to the words of the prophecy of this book, that **"God shall add unto him the plagues"** that are written in this book. **And if any man shall "take away" from the words of the book** of this prophecy, "**God shall take away his part out of the Book of Life,** and out of the holy city, and from the things that are written in this Book" (Revelation 22:18–19).

I believe that warning is not just for the book of Revelation but how we handle all of the Word of God. **God's Word is precious to Him, and it is "settled in heaven." It does not "change.** The Word of God is a **"living document,"** which means it is **"alive" (Hebrews 4:12)**, but unlike the US Constitution—which is said by some to be a "living document," meaning it has to be updated and "amended" (changed)—**the Word of God is "alive," but it does not need to be "amended" or changed.**

Believe it or not, that old KJV Bible that you got ten or fifteen years ago is still good, unless you have worn it out from use, like I have done to a couple of mine. **Wanting to have a more "modern" version such as the New King James Version (NKJV) or wanting a newer Bible because of improved "Bible helps" or an improved layout is understandable and acceptable,** but remember, a "good version" is good for the life of the Bible and does not need to be "updated."

Subtle and overt attacks

Some of these attacks on the Bible or on the Word of God are subtle and some not so subtle (overt). **I said earlier in chapter 8 ("The Attack on the Church") that children are being discouraged from bringing Bibles to public schools.** School teachers and corporate employees are prohibited from displaying Bibles, crosses, and other religious items on their personal desks. Cities and municipalities are removing and restricting displays of the Ten Commandments or any religious symbols. **These are overt attacks on the Bible or on anything Bible based.**

Nowadays, any reference to God or the Holy Bible or any principle put forth in the Bible is frowned upon as **"hate speech"** and is not **"politically correct."** People even want to remove the reference to "God" from the Pledge of Allegiance.

Things have gotten so bad in the United States that **a few years ago, one of our prominent political parties entertained a motion to remove any reference to "God" from their political platform.** The vote "for" or "against" the motion was close; in fact, it was about equal, but I'm glad that the presiding official took the liberty to keep a reference to "God" in their platform. **If God ain't in it, I don't want anything to do with it.**

This attack on the Word of God or anything godly is not a new phenomenon. **Satan began his attack on the Word of God way back in the garden of Eden.** After God gave Adam His Word and told him not to eat from the fruit of the tree in the middle of the garden, along came satan and started an attack on the Word of God. **In the book of Genesis chapter 3, in the form of a "serpent," satan said to Eve, "Yea has God said you shall not eat of every tree of the Garden?"**

Eve replied, "We may eat of the fruit of the trees of the Garden: But of the fruit of the tree in the midst of the Garden, God has said, You shall not eat of it, neither shall you touch it. Lest you die."

Then the devil actually contradicted God and deceived Eve, telling her, "You shall not surely die" (Genesis 3:1–6).

This was a "subtle" attack on the very Word of God. When God told Adam if they disobeyed Him and ate of the fruit of that tree that they would "surely die," **God meant just what He said.** Adam and Eve disobeyed God and ate of the forbidden fruit, and **they died spiritually right then.** They were immediately separated from God, **and thus, they were "dead."** It just took a little while for physical death to be finalized in their physical bodies.

I am glad that although satan deceived Adam and Eve and caused them to doubt what God had said, **God still**

proclaimed that He would make a way for mankind to get victory over satan. God said, "And I will put enmity between thee and the woman, and between thy seed and her seed; It shall bruise thy head, and thou shall bruise His heel" (Genesis 3:15). **He was talking about Jesus Christ, our Savior (the "seed of the woman"), who would "bruise" the serpent's head (satan) and give us the victory.**

Satan has even deceived some churches, pastors, ministers, and people in general into minimizing and downplaying the significance of the written Word of God. The Holy Bible or the Word of God should be honored, cherished, and revered, especially by the church. **Remember, it is "the Word of God," and it is "forever settled in heaven" (Psalm 119:89).**

The Word of God is the one thing that the Church or anybody else can stand on and have full assurance that it's not going to change. **Jesus Christ said, "Heaven and earth shall pass away but My words shall not pass away" (Matthew 24:35).**

Jesus also said in Matthew 7:24–25,

> **Therefore whosoever heareth these sayings of Mine, and doeth them, I will liken him unto a wise man,** which built his house upon a rock. And the rain descended, and the floods came, and the winds blew, and beat upon that house; and it fell not: for it was founded upon a rock.

On the contrary, He said in verses 26–27,

> **And everyone that heareth these sayings of Mine, and doeth them not, shall be likened unto a foolish man,** which built his house upon the sand. And the rain descended, and the floods came, and the winds blew, and beat upon that house; and it fell: and great was the fall of it.

The best foundation that the Church or any human being can have is the Word of God, so we need to stand on the Word if we want to have God's reassurance.

Following the Bible or "standing on the Word" can be as simple as practicing biblical principles such as men removing their caps or head coverings when they are praying or in worship, as instructed in **1 Corinthians 11:4.** I've been around some local pastors who don't practice that or teach it in complete disregard for the Scriptures.

I've also seen some church services on television where **men were wearing caps and hats right in front of the pastor while he was preaching or praying over them, again in complete disregard for the Word of God**, as if he didn't know the Word or just didn't care to practice it or teach it. Jesus said, **"Whosoever shall break one of the least of these commandments, and shall teach men so, he shall be called the least in the kingdom of heaven" (Matthew 5:19a).** If we want to please God and be highly esteemed of God, we must practice and teach His Word.

The importance and significance of the Word of God

If the "world" doesn't respect the Bible, the Church should. **Our faith in God comes from the Holy Bible, which is the "Word of God."** Our faith does not come from just anywhere or from foolishness or out of "thin air." Real faith is rooted and grounded in the Word of God. **"So then faith cometh by hearing, and hearing by the Word of God" (Romans 10:17).**

If you have any faith in God, it has to come from your reading the written Word **(*Logos*)**; or hearing someone speak the Word ("preach" it); or God, by the Spirit, may have **spoken** it to you or revealed it to you Himself **(a *Rhema* word).** The Scripture says, "How then shall they call on Him in whom they have not believed? **And how shall they believe in Him in whom they have not heard?** And how shall they hear without a preacher?" (Romans 10:14). **That's how we got faith in God. We heard somebody "preach" the Word of God.** The preacher needs to "preach the Word" of God.

The Bible, which is the Word of God, will lead us and guide us into all truths when we properly interpret it and when we are being led by the Holy Spirit. **The psalmist said, "Thy Word is a lamp unto my feet, and a light unto my path" (Psalm 119:105).**

The Word of God has liberating and enlightenment power. Jesus said, "If you continue in My Word, then are you My disciples indeed; And you shall know the truth, and the truth shall make you free" (John 8:31–32).

The Word of God should unite us and cause us to be on "one accord." If we use a "good Bible" and if we stand on it and abide in it, the Word of God will bring us together into the "unity of the faith." **That's one of the functions of the fivefold ministry, "Till we all come into the unity of the faith" (Ephesians 4:13).**

We need to understand that no matter how much we study and toil in the Word, we are not going to fully understand everything that is written in the Bible. Apostle Paul said, "For now we see through a glass darkly; but then face to face: Now I know in part; but then I shall know even as also I am known" (1 Corinthians 13:12). **In the words of the old Church hymn, "We'll understand it better by and by."**

Satan knows the importance of the Word of God. That's why he tries to undermine it and turn everybody against it. **He knows that our salvation, our liberation, our unity, and our blessings are dependent upon us "abiding" in the Word of God.** In fact, that's how we prove to be a "disciple indeed."

Jesus said, "If you continue in My Word, then are you My disciples indeed; And you shall know the truth and the truth shall make you free" (John 8:31–32). **Continuing in the Word of God is how we prove to be "a disciple indeed" or a true disciple.**

Because of the significance of the Holy Bible and what it represents, we should fight to keep the Bible as a prominent and prevalent part of our churches, our homes, and in the public square. The public square is where it gets most difficult and challenging, but remember, we are not supposed to be discriminated against because of our religion. **We have a constitutional right to "freedom of religion" (Amendment I, US Constitution).**

Fighting for the sanctity and reverence of the Holy Bible means that we must continue to practice biblical principles and precepts, even while applying them to "modern times," because the Bible does not "change." **The book of Jude tells us that we should "earnestly contend for the faith that was once delivered unto the saints" (Jude verse 3).** Remember, that's where our faith comes from!

Chapter 10

The Attack on the Family

Ever since the very creation of mankind, satan has been constantly launching an attack against the family unit. After Adam and Eve yielded to the temptation of the devil and sinned against God, man took on a "sin nature," and that sin nature was passed down to every human being through the "seed" of Adam.

That sin nature was manifested in Cain, the firstborn son of Adam and Eve, when the devil, working through him, caused him to become jealous and slay his brother, Abel (Genesis 4:1–10). **Of course, this disrupted the peace, harmony, and unity of the "first family."**

Cain's slaying of his brother caused him to be cursed and to never be able to reap a full harvest from his "tilling of the ground." **Cain had to leave the family unit of Adam and Eve**, and from that point on, he would become a "fugitive and a vagabond in the earth" (Genesis 4:11–12).

Satan is still attacking the family unit today. Why do you think we see so much turmoil and disharmony in the family? **In fact, it seems like satan has increased**

his attacks over the last fifteen to twenty years and has become more aggressive when dealing with the family.

Marriage (revisited)

Satan begins his attack with marriage, which was the first "institution" established by God. After God created the man and the woman (Adam and Eve), He performed the first marriage ceremony and joined them together in "holy matrimony." "Therefore shall a man leave his father and his mother, and shall cleave unto his wife: and they shall be one flesh" (Genesis 2:24).

Since its inception in Genesis 2:24 and at least up to the twentieth century (1900s), marriage has been revered, cherished, and highly esteemed by civilized cultures of all nations. Here in the United States, young men and young women used to look forward to getting married, and once they were married, they fought hard to keep their marriage together.

Not anymore! **Along came the twenty-first century, and it looks like satan has stepped up his attack on marriage.** Nowadays, people are just as likely to **"shack up"** as they are to get married. I know that people has been "shackin'" down through the years, but it has now become a **"norm"** and an acceptable lifestyle, especially in the secular world.

I agree with Dr. Ed Young, a prominent evangelical pastor, when he said, "Marriage is the foundation upon which all of humanity stands." Unfortunately, even "church folks" are putting less and less emphasis on marriage and are beginning to get divorces or cohabit or shack up just like the world. **According to statistics by The Barna Group, Christians are engaging in divorces at about the same rate as non-Christians (at thirty-two percent of marriages ending in divorce versus thirty-three percent, respectively).**

Satan fights hard to discourage, disrupt, and break up marriages, so instead of marrying, people will just shack up and avoid the responsibilities of marriage while losing the blessings of God that come along with marriage. Attacking marriages and causing people to devalue marriage just go to show that the devil is busy in his attack on the family, but the Bible tells us that **"Marriage is honorable in all, and the bed undefiled: but whoremongers and adulterers God will judge" (Hebrews 13:4)**.

Absentee dads

A lot of households today are "headed" by single mothers. The man or the "father" is becoming less and less present in the home, and we are seeing more of what is known as **absentee-dad** situations. This is sad when it comes to the biblical model and the survival and the well-being of "the family."

In chapter 8, I noted that **God had ordained a "hierarchy"** that was to continue in marriage. God has ordained that the man have the "position of authority" in the Church and in the home or in the marriage relationship. **When the man is "absent" in the home or in the family, it opens**

that home or that family up to being more vulnerable to the attacks of the devil.

I know that a lot of single mothers, for whatever reason, because of the absence of their child's father, are having to perform head-of-household duties. **I must commend them for doing an excellent job under the circumstances, but in order to raise a child efficiently and properly, it really takes two parents, a "mother" and a "father" (biblically, a husband and a wife).** It took a man and a woman to conceive that child, and it takes a man and a woman to raise the child properly. **God made it that way.**

So when the man is "absent," it leaves the family or the home more vulnerable to a satanic attack. **Jesus said in Matthew 12:29, "Or else how can one enter into a strong man's house, and spoil his goods, except he first bind the strong man? And then he will spoil his house."**

Just like He did with Adam, God ordained for the man to be the "strong man" of the house, and He is holding the man accountable. When the devil is able to "bind" the man and cause him to be "absent" in the family or in the home, then he will come in and "spoil" the home or wreck the family.

God holds marriage and the family in the highest regard. In fact, the **Church as an "institution" is actually second to marriage and the family.** That's why when speaking of marriage, Jesus said, "What therefore God has joined together, let not man put asunder" (Matthew 19:6b).

When speaking about bishops over the church, **Apostle Paul said that a bishop must first rule his own house well:** "For if a man know not how to rule his own house, how shall he take care of the church of God?" (1 Timothy 3:5). **God places high priority on the family.**

Gay or homosexual marriage (revisited)

Along with the deterioration of the family, it appears that satan has launched an all-out attack on marriage and the family unit as God had ordained for it to be. **Again, as I noted in chapter 8, some churches accept the gay or homosexual lifestyle as being an acceptable practice.** Not only are they performing gay marriages, but they are ordaining gay ministers and gay priests and are setting them up to be over the congregation in the churches.

This is what the Bible calls "heresy," a complete departure from sound biblical teaching (2 Peter 2:1). It is a blatant attack upon the institution of marriage and the family structure as God has ordained it to be. **Please have another look at chapter 8 under the heading "Gay or homosexual lifestyles" for the scriptural opposition to the homosexual lifestyle.**

This is another attempt by the devil to undermine the institution of marriage, degrade and confuse the role of the man, and destroy the family. **The "don't ask, don't tell" policy initiated by then-president Bill Clinton in the 1990s just wasn't enough, and permitting "same sex civil unions" wasn't enough.** Satan will not be satisfied until he has corrupted, perverted, or destroyed everything that is godly. **That is his mission, "to steal, kill and destroy" (John 10:10).**

Gay marriage weakens the institution of marriage because now, with gay marriage, you have two women living together as "husband and wife" or two men living together as "husband and wife." **This is confusion.** In fact, the Bible calls it a **"reprobate mind"** (Romans 1:28).

God made it possible for "natural" and "unnatural" desires to be brought under control through a spiritual experience, which Jesus Christ called being "born again." **He said, "Except a man be born again he cannot see the kingdom of God" (John 3:3).** Being born again helps us control both heterosexual and homosexual desires, **but the Bible simply does not condone homosexual relationships.**

There is a reason why God, in His infinite wisdom, made us "male and female" (Matthew 19:4). God made us so that a woman cannot conceive without a man, and a man cannot have children without a woman. **Gay couples cannot procreate through their sexual relationship because it is an unnatural and an ungodly relationship.**

Just because something is "legal" does not mean that it is "holy and acceptable unto God." Children being brought up in a gay environment are going to be confused. If they are not sure about their sexual identity and **if they're taught that its acceptable, of course they're going to be "open" to the gay lifestyle.** That's what's happening in our schools, universities, and throughout the United States, and even our churches have been seduced into going right along with the degradation of society.

Yes, we should "love" everybody and treat everybody right (the way we want to be treated)—whether

they are White, Black, gay, or "straight"—but we cannot condone everything that everybody wants to do. Encouraging or enabling an ungodly or detrimental lifestyle is not true *agape* love.

The Bible says that "*agape* love," which is called "charity" or "benevolent love," "rejoices not in iniquity, but rejoices in the truth" (1 Corinthians 13:6). When the Bible speaks of "loving one another," it is talking about loving one another with the **"love of God" (*agape* love).** We call it **"in spite of,"** loving a person in spite of who they are or how they may be behaving. *Agape* love is really a "tough love."

A lot of people say they "love God," but they don't honor God or do what God wants them to do. Jesus said, "If you love Me keep My commandments. **If a man love Me, he will keep My words:** and My Father will love him, and We will come unto him, and make our abode with him" (John 14:15, 23).

Loving a person with the love of God does not mean that just anything goes and that we are to be permissive and accept everything that people want to do or let everything go unchecked. **No. On the contrary, it means that we must care enough about people ("charity" or "benevolent love") to tell them the truth** and love them "in spite of" who they are or how they might be behaving.

With just a little bit of reflection and spiritual insight, one can readily see what satan is doing to marriage and the family and ultimately to the Church. **He is distorting the meaning of the "love of God,"** undermining and destroying the institution of marriage, denigrating and "binding" the man of the house, and morally and ethically weakening and confusing our children. No wonder our children are confused.

Think about what the next generation is going to be like. **We need to stand up and fight for the principles and precepts that are given to us in our Bible** so that we can get the victory and be delivered from the evil that has invaded the family and is now invading the Church.

Chapter 11

What We Must Do

If we are to "overcome the evil," we cannot just "roll over" and cooperate with the devil and just let him have his way with us or have his way in situations that we are involved in. **We must identify the evil and recognize that we have an "adversary" (the devil)**, and he is particularly trying to destroy us, the Church, or anyone who will let him.

Jesus said in John 10:10a, "The thief comes only to steal, and to kill, and to destroy," and 1 Peter 5:8 says, "Be sober, be vigilant; because your adversary the devil, as a roaring lion, walketh about seeking whom he may devour." Verse 9 says, **"Whom resist steadfast in the faith, knowing that the same afflictions are accomplished in your brethren that are in the world."**

The Bible tells us in James 4:7, "Submit yourselves therefore to God. Resist the devil and he will flee from you." It does you no good to try to fight and resist the devil if you are not submitted to God. You need to be assured that you are submitted to God yourself and that God is on your side **because satan is stronger than you if you are not submitted to God.**

God tells us how to fight and "resist" the devil. He tells us, **"Put on the whole armor of God**, that you may be able to stand against the wiles of the devil" because He knows that we are engaged in spiritual warfare (Ephesians 6:11-12). **God tells us to "put on" eight pieces of armor:** (1) truth; (2) the breastplate of righteousness; (3) the preparation of the gospel of peace; (4) the shield of faith; (5) the helmet of salvation; (6) the sword of the Spirit, which is the Word of God; (7) prayer; and **(8) watching with all perseverance.**

"Watching" is not usually counted as a part of our armor, but I'm including it because it is important that we be alert and "watch." **A "good soldier" must have on the "whole armor" and be on guard at all times.** Keep your guard up!

Watch and pray

To resist the devil and overcome the evil, we must be alert and on guard. **When praying in the garden of Gethsemane** and getting ready to face the cross, Jesus told His disciples to **"watch and pray that you enter not into temptation:** the spirit indeed is willing, but the flesh is weak" (Matthew 26:41).

As "soldiers on the battlefield," we are told to "be sober [serious], be vigilant; because your adversary the devil, as a roaring lion, walketh about, seeking whom he may devour" (1 Peter 5:8). **If you are not serious and vig-**

ilant, the devil will take advantage of you, taking you captive and having you under his influence, perhaps unbeknownst to you.

The book of Jude reminds us that's how the devil got in and took advantage of the Church in the first place. **We are told,**

> **Earnestly contend for the faith that was once delivered unto the saints. For there are certain men crept in unawares,** who were before of old ordained to this condemnation, ungodly men, turning the grace of our God into lasciviousness, and denying the only Lord God, and our Lord Jesus Christ. (Jude verses 3–4)

Prayer was an integral part of Jesus's life. One of His disciples, after watching Him, recognized the importance of prayer and requested of Jesus, **"Lord, teach us to pray** as John also taught his disciples" (Luke 11:1). **Jesus responded by teaching them that "model prayer" known as "the Lord's Prayer"** (Luke 11:2–4 and Matthew 6:9–13).

In that prayer, take note that two of the requests that Jesus made to Father God were (1) "and lead us not into temptation" and (2) "but deliver us from evil." **These two prayer requests, together with what Jesus prayed in John 17:15 that Thou should "keep them from the evil," inspired the title for this book, *Lord, Deliver Us from the Evil.*** Jesus said being delivered from evil should be part of our requests to God, so that reassures us to know that God wants to deliver us from the evil, but we must want deliverance and need to request it.

Be persistent in prayer

In Luke 18, Jesus gives a great parable on the effectiveness of being persistent in prayer. He begins in verse 1 by saying, "Men ought to always to pray, and not to faint." To be delivered from the devil or the evil affecting us, it's important that we don't "faint" or get weak in our prayer life.

Jesus went on to tell about a widow who took her case to a judge in the city and asked the judge to "avenge me of my adversary." The Bible says, "And he would not for a while." This judge did not want to help this widow because **Jesus called him an "unjust judge."** He decided to help the widow because of her persistence, "lest by her continual coming she wearies me" (Luke 18:2–6).

Because of her persistence, this unjust judge decided to help this widow and give her that which she requested. **Jesus used this parable to show the contrast between the "unjust judge" and a just and loving God.** He says, "Hear what the unjust judge says. And shall not God avenge His own elect, which cry day and night unto Him, though He bears long with them? I tell you He will avenge them speedily" (Luke 18:6–8a).

I know that there are some folks who teach that you only need to pray over something one time. **They say, "Ask God for it once and have faith in God that He heard**

you, and He's going to do it, and don't ask again." That approach is only half true. There are some things that we need to pray about and **ask God for "daily" and sometimes over and over and over again,** such as daily peace, daily protection, and "daily bread." "Give us this day our daily bread" (Matthew 6:11).

Pray until God moves in your situation or gives you an answer or gives you peace, especially if you know that it's His will to do what you're asking him to do. **There is a well-known acronym for this; it's called "PUSH: pray until something happens."**

In the parable noted above, the widow kept coming to the unjust judge because she knew that he had the power to help her even though he didn't want to. **This is a contrast. God is not like the unjust judge. God wants to bless us if we have faith and be persistent.** The Bible says, "It is your Father's good pleasure to give you the kingdom" (Luke 12:32).

Fast and pray

We must get back to having fasting as part of our prayer life and part of our Christian lifestyle. Fasting helps us get control over our flesh as well as over external forces. **Jesus intends for us to both pray and fast.** In Matthew chapter 6, leading up to the Lord's Prayer, He gives instructions on how to pray (Matthew 6:6–8). **Then immediately after teaching the Lord's Prayer, He gives instructions on how to fast.** "Moreover when you fast" (Matthew 6:16–18). Jesus gives us specific instructions on how to fast, and He lets us know that He not only intends for us to pray, but He also intends for us to fast.

In Mark chapter 9, Jesus told His disciples **there was a type of evil spirit (demon) that they would not be able to cast out by prayer alone but by prayer and fasting.** "And He said unto them, "This kind can come forth by nothing, but by prayer and fasting" (Mark 9:29). We need to pray and fast for power over the devil, for deliverance, for spiritual strength, and for "revelation knowledge." **The book of Isaiah, chapter 58,** gives additional instructions on **how to fast an "acceptable fast unto the Lord."**

God said that there is a fast that is unacceptable to Him, and there is a fast that is acceptable to Him. Then God tells us what kind of fast would be acceptable to Him:

> **Is this not the fast that I have chosen?** To loose the bands of wickedness, to undo the heavy burdens, and to let the oppressed go free, and that you break every yoke? Is it not to deal thy bread to the hungry, and that thou bring the poor that are cast out to thy house? When thou see the naked, that thou cover him; and that thou hide not thyself from thine own flesh. (Isaiah 58:6–7)

God said after His people have fasted an acceptable fast unto Him that they will see amazing results. "Then shall thy light break forth as the morning, **and thine health shall spring forth speedily:** and thy righteousness shall go before thee; **the glory of the Lord shall be thy rearward."** (Isaiah 58:8)

For those who think they cannot fast because of medical conditions, taking medications, etc., perhaps the book of Daniel, chapter 10:1–3, will offer some encouragement and directions that should help you. Daniel said, "A thing was revealed" unto him which caused him to go into "mourning three full weeks."

During those three weeks, Daniel "ate no pleasant bread." It was a type of fast where he was selective and ate no food that was "pleasant" to him and drank no "wine" or strong drink. Because of his fasting and praying, **Daniel got the answer to the problem that had been "revealed" to him and also got help from an angel who appeared as a messenger from God.**

The spirit of the fast is what matters to God. If you set aside some designated time to consecrate yourself to God to limit your natural food intake and to dedicate yourself fully and wholly to God, that gets God's attention. **It puts you in a spiritual state where God can minister to you and give you power over your own flesh (self),** which includes at least two of the avenues that satan uses to take advantage of us: "the lust of the flesh, and the lust of the eyes" (1 John 2:16).

Stand up

We should not only "pray and fast," but we should "stand up" for the faith. When we get finished praying about all the wrongs and the evils that are in the world, we should get off our knees and take a "stand" against those evils. **Some folks call it "putting feet to your prayers."**

We should stand up and fight for biblical principles and be careful ("vigilant") **to not become hypocritical or "double minded."** The Bible says, **"A double minded man is unstable in all his ways" (James 1:8).**

Part of our problem today is many of our preachers and ministers of the gospel are not standing up for the Word of God or for the gospel of Jesus Christ. We are not "called" to be popular; **we are called to "preach the Word"** of God (2 Timothy 4:2). We should strive to be part of the solution, not part of the problem.

Many pastors, ministers of the gospel, and church members are simply too quiet when it comes to standing up against the evils that we are confronted with in the world. **I sometimes refer to us (the Church) as "the silent majority."** If the Church would only stand up and speak up, many of the evils and the corruption that are running rampant around us would be bound, minimized, and rendered ineffective, if not totally eliminated.

As I said in chapter 1, when dealing with the temptations of Jesus (Matthew 4:3–10), **satan does not care whether you know scriptures or can quote scriptures** as long as you don't practice the Scriptures properly or stand on what the Word of God says.

One way that we can stand up and speak up is by showing up to vote for godly principles and for God-fearing candidates. Voting is another way of "putting feet to your prayers." Not only should we vote during national, state, and local elections, **but we should be concerned**

about issues that affect our communities, and we should let elected officials know where we stand on the issues. When it comes to the controversial issues, **the Church is quite often too quiet, not heard from and invisible.**

As Christians, we are actually supposed to be seen and heard. Our presence is supposed to be known and felt. Jesus said in Matthew 5:13–16,

> You are the **salt of the earth**… You are the **light of the world. A city that is set on a hill cannot be hid**… Let your light so shine among men, **that they may see your good works and glorify your Father** which is in heaven.

We must make some noise. Don't be afraid or ashamed to stand up for biblical truths and biblical values; **be noisy about it.** On that great day **when Jesus came riding into Jerusalem on a donkey ("Palm Sunday")**, the Bible says that they spread their garments and tree branches in the path for Jesus, and **"the whole multitude of the disciples [including little children] began to rejoice and praise God for all the mighty works that they had seen"** (Luke 19:37).

Some of the Pharisees were offended and told Jesus, "Master, rebuke Thy disciples."

But Jesus answered them and said, **"I tell you that if these shall hold their peace, the stones would immediately cry out"** (Luke 19:40).

I say unto you that we don't need the stones to cry out for us because the Lord has been so good to us that we ought not be ashamed to tell it and be noisy about it.

As we take our stand, we must **remember that we were not called to "change" the Word of God; we were "called" to change the "world."** We must change the world through application of the Word and through preaching, teaching, and being a "witness" of Jesus Christ. **Remember the stern warning to those who would tamper with the Word of God:**

> **If any man shall add** unto these things, **God shall add** unto him the plagues that are written in this Book: And **if any man shall take away** from the words of the Book of this prophecy, **God shall take away** his part out of the Book of Life, and out of the holy city, and from the things which are written in this **Book. (Revelation 22:18–19)**

I believe that applies to the entire Bible.

We must be careful how we engage in politics and other issues that affect us in the world. **Yes, we must be involved in the issues of our day, but we must not let those issues overcome us or move us away from godly or biblical principles.** Jesus prayed to Father God in John 17:15, **"I pray not that Thou should take them out of the world, but that Thou should keep them from the evil."**

We must not become cynical or "sick" in our thinking to the point that we cannot accept facts and truths and apply them fairly and objectively in our evaluation of situations and individuals. **Beware of going along with worldly ideas or popular ideas or "movements" just to be "politically correct."** In Matthew 16:6, Jesus said, **"Take heed and beware of the leaven of the Pharisees and of the Sadducees,"** and in Galatians 5:9, Apostle Paul said, **"A little leaven leaveneth the whole lump."** Leaven is an ingredient added to bread or flour dough, which "lightens" it and causes it to rise or puff up. **In other words, if the Church allows infiltration or contamination from just a few bad outside ideas, after a while, the whole Church or the "whole lump" will be contaminated.**

When Apostle Paul was coming to the end of his life, he wrote to Timothy, saying,

> **I have fought a good fight. I have finished my course. I have kept the faith:** Henceforth there is laid up for me **a crown of righteousness,** which the Lord, the righteous judge, shall give me at that day: **and not for me only, but for all them also that love His appearing. (2 Timothy 4:7–8)**

Christians must stand up and fight, fight for the principles and the truths and the ideals of our faith. **Jude said that we should "earnestly contend for the faith that was once delivered unto the saints" (Jude verse 3).**

No, we're not going to go out and commit violent or destructive acts trying to overcome the evil, but we do need to stand up and **use peaceful, "nonviolent" means, following the model given to us by our Lord Jesus Christ and by the late Rev. Dr. Martin Luther King Jr.** We must strive to be "triumphant and victorious" over the evil that exists in this world and not give in to it and not give up on the battle. **This is one battle that God wants us to fight.**

Remember, God equips us to do spiritual battle in this world, and we fight using our spiritual weapons. **Second Corinthians 10:4** tells us that "the weapons of our warfare are not carnal, but mighty through God to the pulling down of strongholds." **We have powerful spiritual weapons such as prayer, the Word of God, faith (keep the faith), the name Jesus, unity, and the power of the vote.**

Have unity

The church and people of like faith need to stand together in unity. We need to stand united in our fight against satan and the evil that is attacking us. We have biblical principles to fight for and to stand on. One biblical principle tells us that there is power in unity, even when there is only a few of us. **Leviticus 26:8 tells us that "five of you shall chase an hundred, and an hundred of you shall put ten thousand to flight."**

Individually, all of us, through our faith in God and through our relationship with God, **have access to some supernatural power**, but an even more familiar scripture in **Deuteronomy 32:30 lets us know that "one can chase a thousand, and two put ten thousand to flight."** It's all about being united and on one accord and having faith in our God. **Our power is multiplied and amplified through unity.**

One of the tactics of the devil is to get us divided and fighting against each other. Look at what's happening in the world today. We have church folks and people who are supposedly of the same faith fighting against one another. **We are allowing things like politics, racial issues, abortion rights, and gay rights issues to divide us.**

Many of these issues, which we should oppose, would not become the "law of the land" unless smooth politicians and special interest groups can get church folks and "people of faith" to vote for them. Instead of standing up and making sure our voices are heard, sometimes we'll concede biblical principles and vote along with what's popular or "politically correct." **We should insist that these politicians, political parties, and others stand for what we believe in if they want our vote.**

Each individual must take a personal stand for biblical truths, and we must also stand together as an "organized body of believers," united in Christ Jesus and united in the faith of what the Word of God says. **We must be like the "three Hebrews boys" Shadrach, Meshach, and Abednego when they told King Nebuchadnezzar, "Our God whom we serve is able to deliver us, but even if He does not, we will not bow.** We will not serve thy gods nor worship the golden image which thy has set up" (Daniel 3:16–18).

Most folks know the story of how they refused to bow down to the golden image and were cast into the fiery furnace. **Yet they were not harmed**. In fact, King Nebuchadnezzar looked into the fiery furnace and instead of seeing three men, he saw four men, and he proclaimed, **"Lo I see four men…and the form of the fourth is like the Son of God" (Daniel 3:24–25).**

When you're standing on the Word of God, anything that God doesn't save you from, He will be with you in it, and He will keep you even in the time of trouble. **The late congressman and civil rights activist, patriarch, and icon Rev. John Lewis called it "getting into good trouble."**

We should not let minor nuances in the Word of God divide us and keep us from working together in unity. There are some things in the Bible that none of us fully understand. Apostle Paul said, **"For now we see through a glass, darkly;** but then face to face: Now I know in part; but then shall I know even as also I am known" (1 Corinthians 13:12). **In other words, "We'll understand it better by and by."**

If your friends or others have a different understanding than you, **listen to them. Then "try the spirit"** to make sure you are objectively interpreting the Scriptures. As much as possible, try to work out your differences and work together. **Apostle Paul tell us in Ephesians 4:3 to be "endeavoring to keep the unity of the Spirit in the bond of peace."**

Jesus Christ warned us of the danger of being divided when He said, "Every kingdom divided against itself is brought to desolation; **and every city or house divided**

against itself shall not stand" (Matthew 12:25). Can that be the reason why our churches are so ineffective in the world today, because satan has caused us to be divided against one another?

We must stand united on the Word of God and do our best to convince others of the divinity and the inspiration of the Word of God. **We have a mandate from Jesus Christ to do that. It's called "the Great Commission,"** and again, it's found in **Matthew 28:19–20.** The Word of God should unite us more than it divides us.

Chapter 12

Conclusion of the Whole Matter

It is important that we recognize, acknowledge, and resist the evil that is all around us in the world. **Evil is an inherent part of this world,** most of it caused by satan or spiritual forces, but there are some "evils" that may be caused by natural forces. **We should not only be aware of the presence of evil, but we should be aware of the causes of the evil.**

We should also want to be "delivered" from the evil. We should not succumb to the evil and allow it to manipulate us, oppress us, distress us, depress us, or overcome us. **Our Lord and Savior, Jesus Christ, said that deliverance should be part of our prayers** when He taught us to pray, "And lead us not into temptation, but deliver us from evil," in (Matthew 6:13). Then He prayed to Father God to "keep them from the evil" in John 17:15.

We should have a strong prayer life and this request to be delivered should be part of our sincere desire and part of our requests to Father God. **I'm not trying to be pious or "holier than thou" because I know that I hav-**

en't always been "saved." For a number of years, I was living in a "backslidden" state, drinking, partying, gambling, pool sharking, and using profanity profusely. **Satan had thoroughly seduced me and had me under his power.**

What happened to me is not unique to me. It happens to a lot of people. The Bible tells us in **Ephesians 2:2, "Wherein in times past you walked according to the course of this world, according to the power of the prince of the air,** the spirit that now worketh in the children of disobedience."

Satan, "the prince of the power of the air," is the principal source of much of the evil that we face, and he is trying to get us to **backslide** and become destructive and be lost, **and/or cause other people to be destructive and lost.** That is his mission. Jesus calls him a thief and said, "The thief cometh not, but for to steal, and to kill and to destroy" (John 10:10a).

Oh, yes, you can "backslide" and fall away from the grace that is in Jesus Christ. I do not believe that "once you're saved, you're always saved," but I believe that you have to "fight" and hold on to your faith in God. **I believe in the totality of the Scriptures, which include, "But he that shall endure until the end, the same shall be saved" (Matthew 24:13).**

What is deliverance?

We certainly need deliverance from all kinds of evils that we are confronted with in the world. **The word "deliver," as used in the Lord's Prayer in Matthew 6:13, means to**

"draw out"* or *"rescue." *Webster's Illustrated Contemporary Dictionary* says "deliver" means ***"to free from evil or danger, etc."***

Deliverance means (1) you are "drawn out" or removed from the presence of an evil, or (2) the evil is removed from your presence, or (3) you are strengthened to the point that evil is around you, but it has no power over you. **It is not always God's will to physically remove us from the presence of every evil**, but it is His will to give us power over the evil so that it does not subdue us or control us.

You can be "delivered" from evil and yet **be around evil, but it has no power over you.** You can be delivered from nicotine, cigarette smoking, drinking, cursing and using profanity, and be around people who indulge in such behaviors (or worse), but it does not have a negative influence or power over you. **That's deliverance!**

Jesus said, "If you continue in My Word, then are you My disciples indeed; And you shall know the truth, **and the truth shall make you free"** (John 8:31–32). Continuing in His Word will bring us into the knowledge of the truth and make us free. That means free of whatever is vexing you, hindering you, or holding you in bondage. Sometimes, even though your conditions or your circumstances didn't change, **you changed** because you came into the "knowledge of the truth." So act like it. **Now that's deliverance!**

Continuing in Jesus's Word will also prove that we are His "disciples indeed." It's the proof of a true disciple. That's what we want to be. We want to prove to be true disciples, His "disciples indeed."

Apostle Paul said,

> We are troubled on every side, yet not distressed; we are perplexed, but not in despair; Persecuted, but not forsaken; cast down, but not destroyed; Always bearing about in the body the dying of the Lord Jesus, that the life also of Jesus might be made manifest in our body. **For we which live are always delivered unto death for Jesus' sake, that the life also of Jesus might be made manifest in our mortal flesh. (2 Corinthians 4:8–11)**

Apostle Paul went on to say in Philippians 4:11, "Not that I speak in respect of want: for I have learned, in whatsoever state I am, therewith to be content." We must be delivered to the point that we have inner peace and contentment no matter what state we are in or no matter what is going on around us. **That takes a lot of prayer, fasting, and discipline, but it should be our ultimate goal for ourselves if we are going to please God.**

Ultimate deliverance and victory

We must "study to show ourselves approved unto God," learn how to "rightly divide" the Scriptures, "try the spirits" (see chapter 3, "Discerning the Evil"), and "fight a good fight." **We know that in the end, we win because the book of Revelation lets us know that.**

When the "last trumpet sounds" and the church gets "raptured" out in Revelation 10:7 and Revelation 11:15, then we have the ultimate victory and the ultimate deliverance, which is in Christ Jesus **(look again at "The Rapture" in chapter 5 of this book). First** Thessalonians 4:17b says, "And so shall we ever be with the Lord."

After the rapture, we go up to heaven with Jesus Christ to be "arrayed in fine linen, clean and white" **to attend the "marriage supper of the lamb."** "Blessed are they which are called unto the marriage supper of the Lamb" (Revelation 19:7–9).

Immediately after the marriage supper, when we are literally "married" to the Lamb, **we return to the earth with Jesus (the Lamb)** to subdue the earth and to rule it with Him. John said, "And I saw heaven opened, and behold a white horse; and He that sat upon him was called Faithful and True, and in righteousness He does judge and make war" (Revelation 19:11).

We ("Christians, saints of God, believers") follow Him on white horses because remember, 1 Thessalonians 4:17b says that after the rapture, "and so shall we ever be with the Lord." John said, "And the armies which were in heaven followed Him upon white horses, clothed in fine linen, clean and white" (Revelation 19:14).

So we subdue the earth with Jesus and reign with Him a thousand years. **Then Jesus sends one angel.**

> **And he laid hold on the dragon,** that old serpent, which is the devil, and satan **and bound him a thousand years;** And

> cast him into the bottomless pit, and shut him up, and set a seal upon him, that he should deceive the nations no more, until the thousand years should be fulfilled: **and after that he must be loosed a little season.** (Revelation 20:2–3)

How about that! We actually get to spend a thousand years on the earth with Jesus Christ and without the devil or any evil spirits present to tempt or torment us into sinning or doing evil. It'll be like restoration of the garden of Eden before the serpent corrupted it and caused man to sin.

After our "thousand-year millennium" with Christ, the Bible says that "satan shall be loosed out of his prison, and shall go out to deceive the nations" one more time. He will gather the nations together to do battle against the saints of God, **but fire comes down "from God out of heaven and devoured them" (Revelation 20:7–9).**

Revelation 20:10 says, **"And the devil that deceived them was cast into the lake of fire and brimstone, where the beast and the false prophet are,** and shall be tormented day and night forever and ever." **This is the ultimate victory and ultimate deliverance from the devil and the evil that he has caused upon the earth.**

Yes, we are ultimately triumphant and get the victory and the deliverance, which we so earnestly need and desire, but we are also supposed to **be "triumphant and victorious" right down here in this present world**

before the rapture and before "the millennial kingdom" is established.

When Jesus established His Church, He said, "Upon this Rock I will build My Church; and the gates of hell shall not prevail against It." And then He said,

> **And I will give unto thee the keys of the kingdom of heaven:** and whatsoever thou shall bind on earth shall be bound in heaven: and whatsoever thou shall loosed on earth shall be loosed in heaven. (Matthew 16:18–19)

So the Church will prevail because Jesus established Her upon the "Rock" and gave us some "keys." **We need to discover what the "keys of the kingdom of heaven" are and use them.** A little hint would be anything that gives you access to heaven, **such as: the name Jesus, the Word of God, faith in God, and prayer,** just to name a few.

Speaking of prayer, prayer is a powerful key and a powerful weapon. Remember, Jesus told us, "Men ought to always pray and not to faint" (Luke 18:1). **Then He taught us how to pray, saying, "Pray after this manner,** Our Father which art in heaven, Hallowed be Thy name. Thy kingdom come. Thy will be done in earth, as it is in heaven" (Matthew 6:9–10).

He said that we should pray each day for our "daily bread" and that we should pray for the "forgiveness of our sins" as we forgive others. **Then He said that we should pray, "And lead us not into temptation; but deliver us**

from evil: For Thine is the kingdom, and the power, and the glory, for ever. Amen." (Matthew 6:11–13). This is a great prayer to pray, and it is a **"model"** for our prayer life.

Jesus knew that evil was present with us in this world and that we should pray to be delivered from it. If we want to please God, we must have a desire to be "delivered from the evil," and we should make that request known to Father God (not that He doesn't already know, but He said to ask). **We must get up off our knees, exercise our faith, and let Him deliver us** by doing what we are supposed to do. The Scriptures say, **"But without faith it is impossible to please Him: for he that cometh to God must believe that He is, and that He is a rewarder of them that diligently seek Him" (Hebrews 11:6).**

The Church ("Christians, saints of God, believers") are supposed to make a difference in this world. **We are to be the "salt of the earth, the light of the world; a** city that is set on a hill and cannot be hid" (Matthew 5:13–14). We are to love one another with godly love and treat everybody justly with love and compassion. Jesus said, **"By this shall all men know that you are My disciples, if you have love one to another" (John 13:35).**

The prophet Micah said, "He has showed thee, O man, what is good; and what does the Lord require of thee, but to do justly, and love mercy, and to walk humble with thy God?" (Micah 6:8).

So recognize the evil that is present around you. **Keep praying. Keep fighting. "Fight a good fight.** Keep the faith and finish your course." Surely the Lord will deliver you. We can do what the Lord wants us to do, and we can be what the Lord wants us to be. **Solomon, the wisest man to live upon the earth, said in Ecclesiastes 12:13, "Let us hear the conclusion of the whole matter: Fear God, and keep His commandments: for this is the whole duty of man."** Be blessed. Keep the faith, and **be delivered from the evil.**

Thanks and Appreciation

First, I want to thank God, who blessed me down through the years and inspired me to write this book. I thank Him for blessing me to be able to put my thoughts together and organize this book in such a way that, hopefully, it is easy to read, easy to follow, and easy to understand.

Secondly, I want to thank my wife, Shirley, who has been very supportive throughout the process of preparing this book for publication. Thank God for her invaluable critiques and suggestions along the way. One piece of advice that she gave me that I was always mindful of was, "Keep it brief. Don't write a long book." I guess she was thinking of some of my sermons, so I took extra care to not belabor any points.

Thirdly, I want to thank my two sons, Dr. Clifford Emmanuel Little and Timothy James Little, who took the time to review my work and offer their suggestions. Emmanuel offered some scholarly suggestions for improvement in the manuscript, and I don't know what I would have done without technological assistance from Timothy. When it comes to technology, I'm an old "dinosaur" and not very tech savvy, so his assistance has been absolutely instrumental.

Thanks to my good friend Pastor Robert Johnson, whom I was stationed with in Myrtle Beach, South Carolina, while in the United States Air Force. Robert himself is the author of two very fine books (*The Spirit of the Anti-Christ* and *On Point!: The Making of a Prison Contraband Captain*). Consequently, when I shared with him that I was preparing a book for publication, he was able to give me a number of invaluable suggestions and pointers gained from his own experiences.

A special "thanks" also to my good friend Dr. John M. Dunaway. I am so thankful that he was willing to review this book and thought it was worthy of a foreword from Him. John's establishing of the Beloved Community Paired Clergy Initiative has been instrumental in helping our community overcome racism and move us closer to fulfilling Dr. King's dream of a "beloved community." Thanks again, John, for your notable suggestions and heartfelt statement of support.

Last but not least is Evangelist Debra Harvey, who sat under my pastoral leadership for years. She went on to serve in other ministries in Augusta, Georgia, and today is an anointed, gifted evangelist and a published author herself. Her book and accompanying journal *A Heart Under Surveillance* is an inspiring and encouraging work from the heart. Her willingness to take the necessary time to add her support to this book is much appreciated by me. May she continue in the blessings, peace, and prosperity of the Lord.

Most of the folks noted here offered suggestions for improvement, so if this book doesn't appeal to your liking, blame them. But on a serious note, I followed many of their suggestions but tried to make sure that the substance and the ideas were true to what I believe God gave me to write, so I thank all of them because without them, the completed work would not be possible. **I also thank you, the reader, and I pray that this book is an inspiration and a blessing to you as we all strive to be "delivered from the evil"** while we are living in this world. **Keep the faith. Keep praying and keep fighting to get the victory over the evil. May God bless you real good.**

Your brother in Christ,
Rev., Dr. (Honorary) Clifford Little
Pastor, minister of the gospel

About the Author

Rev. Clifford Little is a Christian preacher who was born in the country area of Twiggs County (no pun intended), just outside of Macon, Georgia. He grew up on a small "patch" farm and had a strict Christian upbringing.

Except for about ten years of his young adult life, Clifford has always been affiliated with the Christian Church. In 1977, he met and married Shirley, the love of his life, who also would become a minister of the gospel. In 1985, he was called to preach, and as a devout, Bible-believing, God-fearing Christian, he devoted himself to the study and understanding of God's Word as stated in the Holy Bible.

Although he took advantage of many personal growth opportunities at various institutions, such as Morris College School of Religion (Sumter, South Carolina) and Emmanuel Bible College (Macon, Georgia), much of his knowledge of God's Word is self-taught through much study and prayer.

Rev. Little loves the Lord, loves the Word of God, and loves God's people. He is the pastor of Green's Tabernacle Baptist Church of Macon, Georgia, and he is concerned about the spiritual well-being as well as the physical well-being of the entire Body of Christ. He is also keenly aware of and concerned about the many evils confronted by Christians and non-Christians in the world today. That is why he wrote this book, to try to help somebody overcome the evils that we are faced with in this world.

Clifford Little, born July 14, 1949 in Twiggs County, Jeffersonville, Georgia, to the parentage of the late Frank Little Jr. and the late Lucille King Little.

Elementary, high school education

- Chance Hill Elementary School
- Antioch Elementary School
- Graduated from Jeffersonville High School in 1967

College education

- Fort Valley State College (now Fort Valley State University)
- Community College of the US Air Force
- Noncommissioned Officer Academy Distinguished Grad, Tyndall AFB, Florida
- Morris College School of Religion, Sumter, South Carolina
- Emmanuel Bible College, Macon, Georgia
- Macon State College (now Middle Georgia State University)
- Georgia College and State University, Macon Campus for Marketing

Ministerial credentials

- "Called" into the gospel ministry by the calling of Jeremiah 1:3–5 (1985)
- Licensed to preach the gospel (January 1986)
- Ordained as a gospel minister (April 1988)
- Former president of the Baptist Ministers Union of Macon, Georgia and vicinity (2005 and 2006)
- Former president of the Evangelical Ministers Alliance of Macon, Georgia and vicinity (2010 and 2011)
- Pastor of Green's Tabernacle Baptist Church, Macon, Georgia (1992–present)
- Received an Honorary Doctorate of Christian Theology Degree from the School of the Great Commission Bible College of Columbia, South Carolina, September 2021

Family affiliations

Married to Evangelist Shirley Jean Little from Charleston, South Carolina; has two sons (Dr. C. Emmanuel Little and Timothy James Little), one daughter-in-law (Crystal), and one very cute and precious granddaughter (Camryn), whom I think we have all spoiled

Vietnam veteran and US Air Force retiree after twenty years of honorable military service (March 1970 to April 1990).

www.ingramcontent.com/pod-product-compliance
Lightning Source LLC
LaVergne TN
LVHW041158070125
800367LV00010BA/269
9781639032761